STRONG ENOUGH
TO BE A MAN

RECLAIMING GOD'S PLAN FOR MASCULINITY

TIM RITER

Beacon Hill Press of Kansas City
Kansas City, Missouri

Copyright 2005
by Tim Riter and Beacon Hill Press of Kansas City

ISBN 083-412-1883

Printed in the
United States of America

Cover Design: Kevin Williamson

Library of Congress Cataloging-in-Publication Data

Riter, Tim, 1948-
  Strong enough to be a man : reclaiming God's plan for masculinity / Tim Riter.
    p. cm.
  ISBN 0-8341-2188-3 (pbk.)
  1. Men (Christian theology). 2. Christian men—Religious life. I. Title.

  BT703.5.R58 2005
  248.8'42—dc22

                        2005012339

10 9 8 7 6 5 4 3 2 1

CONTENTS

INTRODUCTION
MEN ADRIFT

MY DAD KNEW HOW TO BE A MAN. Strong and decisive, he lived the motto "Seldom wrong but never in doubt." He compassionately defended his family and provided for them. He grew up in a broken home; his own father abandoned the family soon after it became a family. But he learned about manhood from living with his extended family, especially his grandfather. Even the society presented a pretty consistent picture of what it meant to be a man.

I grew up watching Dad, Ward Cleaver of *Leave It to Beaver*, Robert Young of *Father Knows Best*; they all presented a heroic, noble vision of manhood. They were good people, doing their best. They were kind, rational, and loving—the kind of man I decided I wanted to become.

BROKEN ROLE MODELS

Then my world changed. And with it, my ideas of masculinity and my role models did as well. Confusion about male and female roles, identities, and natures bombarded us, starting in the mid-1960s and continuing into the 21st century. No one quite knows anymore what it means to be a man.

The sexual revolution taught us to seek pleasure as much as we can, wherever we can. The halftime "show" at the 2004 Super Bowl showed us far more of Janet Jackson than we could have imagined back in the days of Robert Young. Even as I researched this section, a graphic ad popped up on my screen, letting me know that nothing should interfere with receiving pleasure. Several celebrities revealed their pledges to be celibate until marriage, but some of them later became extremely sexually expressive. How do godly men face this abundance of sexual temptation?

The feminist movement tried to deny any differences between men and women. Boys played with trucks because we gave them trucks; girls played with dolls because we gave them dolls. Feminists encouraged men to seek out "their feminine side," and masculine strength was decried as "macho posturing."

Television transformed itself from *Father Knows Best* to *Married with Children*. Men were portrayed as bumbling incompetents, unable to understand women or to meet their needs. Even shows with basically decent people, like *Home Improvement,* featured men who yearned for "more power" but caused disasters when they got it.

But secularism provided the greatest change in my world. Until roughly the mid-1960s, males grew up in a culture that acknowledged the Judeo-Christian ethic as the basis for morality. Obviously not all followed it, but we shared a common foundation. Secularism took that away, and our society has lost its shared sense of morality. Each individual decides for himself or herself now. I teach communication in a Christian university and recently gave an assignment to develop a biblical base for ethical communication. In the class discussion that led up to that, the students consistently stated that subjective ethics are the best— each individual should choose his or her own ethical pathway.

So how can we Christian men determine the right way to express our manhood? Who sets the rules? The government consistently shows itself a captive of special interests, and laws change from year to year. Society itself has different standards, depending on which region you live in. As I write this, San Francisco offers marriage licenses to homosexual couples, even though California as a state earlier passed an initiative defining marriage as the union between one man and one woman.

Many boys learn ethics from their families, but in our secular culture different families have radically different ethics. A neighbor teaches his son to do whatever he can to get ahead— lie to people, deceive them, or bully them if it benefits him. That neighbor child learns that the highest ethic is self-advancement regardless of the cost to others.

Many of us rely on our emotions to provide direction. I recently heard someone say that a woman should "follow her mother's heart." But I read countless news stories of mothers who abused their children, even drowned them, because their hearts had been captured by romance or depressed by despair.

Even churches struggle; some affirm that homosexual marriage is entirely acceptable, while others define it as sinful. If our spiritual sources contradict one another, then we men find it difficult to develop a clear sense of manhood, of ethics.

Men over the age of 40 share my experience of absorbing two radically different sources of determining masculinity. But men under 40 usually only receive what I did in the second phase. They have few role models of healthy masculinity, so a host of healthful and unhealthful options have jumped into the vacuum.

We have "Iron John" recommending we howl at the moon. John Eldredge wisely encourages us to acknowledge and develop our risky nature. Promise Keepers tapped into men's yearning for spirituality and closeness to God, effectively recognizing the heart cry of men for authentic masculinity and intimacy with God.

This book offers another option to men in our society, one very compatible with Eldredge and Promise Keepers, an option that transcends the many definitions our culture has of manhood.

CHARACTER COUNTS

Character stands at the very heart of masculinity. We may *do* what some say men should, we may *discipline* ourselves to become better men, but more deeply needed than these changes is the transformation of our inward beings. Godly character flows from the heart of God, and we can find no better role model for manhood than the person and nature of God. God expresses the best in manliness.

Obviously, God also expresses the best in womanliness, because the image of God innate to humanity involves both genders. "God created man [humanity] in his own image, in the image of God he created him; male and female he created them" (Gen. 1:27). Intriguingly, we get the best perspective on what the image of God means when looking at both male and female.

We see other aspects of the "feminine side" of God, such as when Jesus pictured himself as a mother hen in Matt. 23:37—"O Jerusalem, Jerusalem, you who kill the prophets and stone those sent to you, how often I have longed to gather your children together, as a hen gathers her chicks under her wings, but you were not willing."

But here we want to focus on God as Father, the perfect father, not like so many absentee, abusive, unfaithful, and workaholic dads who fill the landscape of our lives and provide such anemic role models.

So how do we develop manly character? By nurturing the character of God our Father. How do we do that? The nine dimensions of the fruit of the Spirit listed in Gal. 5:22-23 reveal nine traits of God's character. As we nurture both the presence of the Spirit and each trait, we'll find ourselves in the process of transformation. We'll imbed essential masculinity into our core.

I'm convinced that strength defines maleness. As we couple our innate strength with God's, as we commit to develop these traits of manly character, then we'll reclaim who God created us to be—men.

And He created us to be not just men who act in love but men who have love deeply imbedded in our hearts. Not just men who sometimes act with joy but men who can consistently face the trials of life and respond in joy. Not just men sometimes at peace in the midst of our battles but men who have an inner tranquility despite the pace of life. Not just men who sometimes hang in there but men who don't quit when life seems terminal. Not just men who sometimes act in kindness but men who have kindness that goes clear down to the bone. Not just men who struggle with choosing right and wrong but men who cherish goodness. Not just men who stay married but men who keep all their commitments regardless of the cost. Not just men who demonstrate strength but men who can harness that with gentleness. Not just men who get torn in different directions but men who have the character to do what's right.

Gal. 5:16-26 marvelously details what it means to have God's character grow within us. The goal is given in verses 22-23:

> The fruit of the Spirit is love, joy, peace, patience, kindness, goodness, faithfulness, gentleness, and self-control. Against such things there is no law.

Each of those nine aspects represents a different trait of God's character. When God lives within us through His Holy Spirit, His character transfers itself to ours. That happens as we allow the Spirit to lead each part of our lives. God's character becomes imbedded in ours and expresses itself in our Christian character traits.

This book shows men how to cultivate the fruit of the Spirit. We'll learn how to develop the character of God deep down so that others see the result. The following chapters will examine each expression of God's character so we can learn the specific changes the Spirit makes in our character.

Let's begin the adventure of building manly character.

1
BEYOND OURSELVES

THE MANLY TRAIT OF LOVE

The fruit of the Spirit is love.
Galatians 5:22

PARTICULARLY ON FISHING TRIPS, my dad was both my role model and my greatest rival. Despite our friendly competition, I learned from the expert how to "think like a trout." To this day, I've not seen anyone match Dad on a trout stream. After years of fishing with him, I finally came close to matching him when I found a decent fishing hole. But when the trout had little interest in biting, he kept pulling them out. I never could figure out his secret!

Our bonding on fishing trips increased through our competition in catching the most and largest trout. On a late-fall trip to the Sierras, I was as full of myself as a 16-year-old could be. I drifted a worm along an undercut bank on Oak Creek. The line stopped, but I could feel no tug on the monofilament cradled between my thumb and forefinger to indicate a bite. I pulled the line out of the water to try again, but it just stayed there. I gave a yank, thinking it had gotten snagged on a root.

Slowly the "root" gave way, with the largest trout I had ever seen breaking the surface before it let go. The head alone seemed as big as most trout. My heart stopped. My body just quivered. I gradually composed myself, waited a few moments for the trout to settle down as well, and floated the line past the hole again. It just kept moving. That worm was well drowned before I acknowledged that this trout had quit biting.

Hours later, Dad and I came back to the spot, and I described the whale. I put in to the hole; Dad just chuckled from the other side of the stream.

"Tim, you didn't get a bite. Your line is hung up on a root—you're not even in the water."

Dad was right about the root but wrong about the fish. Just a few seconds later, a rainbow trout erupted from the hole, bending my fly rod double. Once he was over the bank, I pounced like a cougar. This guy wasn't going to fall back in.

He was 16 inches of beauty, coming in at 1½ pounds, huge for a stream just four feet wide. He was even bigger for a young man anxious to prove himself as a true fisherman to his dad. I was filled with pride and accomplishment; I had never seen even Dad catch one this big on a stream.

The euphoria lasted into the next day as we moved over to the creek on the south, Independence. We were fishing 20 feet apart. Then Dad cautiously backed out of his hole and called me over.

"There's a nice one in there. He quit biting for me; maybe you can get him. Just let your line drop over the waterfall. He'll strike when it hits the surface, if he's going to."

Just as deliberately, I slipped into place. Letting out just three feet of line, I watched as the worm went over the falls. Bam! Another lunker. This one measured just a little less than the first, 15½ inches, just a shade under 1½ pounds.

Knowing Dad's competitive nature and fishing prowess, I was suspicious and gave him a gentle put-down. "I bet you knew this guy was just a little smaller, and you didn't want to miss catching the largest fish by so little, did you?"

Dad smilingly denied it, but for years I teased him for giving up such a nice trout. Only years later, after his death, did I finally realize what he had done.

Yes, Dad knew it was a big one. He couldn't help knowing that. And no, the fish didn't quit biting for him. As soon as my worm hit the water, he struck hard. He was hungry. He would have bitten on a rose hip.

But Dad knew this trout might surpass mine from the day before. And he didn't want to risk catching a bigger trout than his son's catch of a lifetime. Dad offered a tremendous act of love, unappreciated for years, until it was too late to acknowledge.

Doing what my dad did is difficult for most men. Sacrificial giving goes against our grain. God calls it love, getting beyond ourselves. Not many men do that easily.

More typical than Dad's act would be that of a certain minister. After years of training and experience, he left the ministry to practice medicine, saying, "I've discovered that people will pay more money to take care of their bodies than to take care of their souls." After several more years, he made another career change, this time to the legal profession. His reasoning? "I've discovered that people will pay more to get their own way than they will to take care of either body or soul."

OUR NATURAL TENDENCY: SELF-ABSORPTION

That story reveals not just the motives of the former minister but the motives of most people. We tend to look at life through our own perspectives. "I'm persistent, but you're pigheaded. I'm convinced, but you're stubborn. I'm flexible, but you're wishy-washy."

For most of us, our own needs are paramount. I struggled with that in my early 20s. If we dropped our concern for our own needs on a balance scale with concern for others on the opposite end, concern for others would be launched to the moon. Obviously, examples of selfless behavior and great sacrifice abound. All of us do some very good things with no expectations of benefit to ourselves.

But we still look at life through the "What's best for me?" filter. Marketing people recognize that. Our innate nature is reinforced by unneeded encouragements to "Have it *your way*," "You *deserve* a break today," and "Who said you can't *have it all*?" Why do they stress these attitudes? Because they've learned that we respond to them. Those statements resonate with something deep within us.

The apostle Paul recognized that we men continue to struggle with that innate trait even after coming to Christ. Writing to Christians, he said, "Everyone looks out for his own interests, not those of Jesus Christ" (Phil. 2:21).

The many exceptions merely prove the truth of this rule. Paul wrote this nearly 2,000 years ago. We haven't improved much in the last two millennia. We still battle the desire for pre-eminence, power, and position.

Read through the gospels to learn how often the apostles argued over who was greatest. When Jesus caught them, they showed appropriate embarrassment, but they still continued to bicker off and on until the very end of Jesus' ministry. Even at the Last Supper, Peter boasted that he alone would remain true to Christ. To Peter, Peter was the best disciple.

We men see that same trait in our own hearts. We have scattered victories, but we all tend to let *self* possess us. We rarely get beyond ourselves. We put our desires at the forefront of our minds.

THE MANLY CHARACTER TRAIT OF LOVE

How does our Christianity impact that innate masculine trait of self-concern? When God's character becomes imbedded in ours, then which of His traits touches our self-centeredness?

Because the issue is so pivotal, the first area God usually transforms in us deals with helping us get beyond ourselves, where we learn to balance our own genuine needs with compassion for others. Why else would love be listed as the first expression of the character of God within? When God comes into our lives, we finally have both the motivation and power to get beyond the trap of self.

Moving away from that preoccupation with our own concerns is the Christian character trait of love. God provides love as an antidote to selfishness.

LOVE DEFINED

But we need to know what God means by love. Our society seems to define love as "a feeling you feel when you feel you've never felt that feeling before." Too frequently we men associate love with lust. Is that the love God wants to incorporate in us? Let me share a working definition of love, and then we'll examine the scriptural examples to show how God loves.

Love is an inner valuing of another that causes you to act in the best interests of the person you love.

First, love is a deep-seated character trait that comes from your attitude about the person you love. You don't value that person because of his or her lovable nature or sinless perfection, but on the fact God loves and values the person.

That inner commitment isn't a mere feeling. Feelings come and go, based on how much sleep you got the night before or the person's last behavior toward you. Love based on feelings is a roller coaster ride, with great highs, great lows, and always a great deal of fear mixed with exhilaration.

That inner character of love values others as much as you value yourself. That value will then result in specific, intentional action, based on what's best for the other person spiritually, emotionally, and physically. You commit yourself to helping that person become who God designed him or her to be.

This doesn't mean you cave in to all of his or her desires. You don't allow him or her to escape responsibility for decisions. But you do interrupt your self-centered agenda, get beyond self-absorption, and become a positive influence in that person's life.

EXAMPLES OF GOD'S LOVE

God loves by acting for your best. Think about Rom. 5:8—"God demonstrates his own love for us in this: While we were still sinners, Christ died for us."

While we were sinners (certainly not deserving of great love), God acted out of His inner character of love (it had to be demonstrated) by sending His Son to die for us (observable, practical action for our spiritual benefit). Because love filled God's character, He acted for our best, at His own cost. Add to this John 3:16—"God so loved the world that he gave his one and only Son, that whoever believes in him shall not perish but have eternal life."

Not Emotions

Once again, God's character of love resulted in actions for the benefit of mankind. Those verses said nothing about God's feelings toward us. If you combine His holiness with our repeated sinfulness, God's feelings could very well have ranged from disgust to anger and disappointment.

But feelings don't drive God. His inner love does. Because God loves, He acts. In the "love chapter," 1 Cor. 13, decide if the description of love refers to feelings or to actions.

Love is patient, love is kind. It does not envy, it does not boast, it is not proud. It is not rude, it is not self-seeking, it is not easily angered, it keeps no record of wrongs. Love does not delight in evil but rejoices with the truth. It always protects, always trusts, always hopes, always perseveres. Love never fails (*1 Cor. 13:4-8*).

Learn What Love Is

Love is imbedded in God's character. All He does flows from love. For us to learn what love means, we need to commit ourselves to the study of God. This chapter provides a start on learning how God acts toward people.

The entire Bible provides the world's best manual on love. Forget Masters and Johnson, the Kama Sutra, and *Playboy*. In the Bible we see how love flows from God's character into His behavior. I encourage you to spend some significant time reading the Bible and looking for just that one thing.

Discover the extent of His love: the number of people who can receive it. Notice the depth: how far God goes in His love. Determine the actions of love: the things God does to demonstrate love. Uncover how His love ends: the fact that nothing we do keeps God from loving us.

Some passages we all know. The love chapter of 1 Cor. 13. The letter of 1 John, where in five brief chapters a form of the word "love" is used about 46 times. But don't miss less obvious passages such as Genesis 1—3. Find the wonderful and loving gift of Eden, and then marvel at the love that prompted the promise of a Redeemer to overcome the effects of humanity choosing sin.

Examine in Gen. 12 the story of God calling Abram, revealing God's desire that "all peoples on earth will be blessed" (v. 3)—not just the chosen people, the Jews, but all. Study the Book of Judges, how frequently God's people left and betrayed Him but how in love He always waited for them to turn around.

Get a good exhaustive concordance and find more passages

about love. Be selective, though. My computer Bible program lists "love" more than 830 times. That study would take days!

Read the Bible to learn the ways the God who lives within us loves. Then you can begin to incorporate that trait of God's into your own character.

CULTIVATING THE MANLY CHARACTER TRAIT OF LOVE

Self-absorption works against love by convincing you that your needs, fears, desires, and preferences come first. That's natural. Just look at "innocent infants." You can't find more selfish creatures—they assume that the world revolves around them. Only the selfishness of some grown men and women exceeds that of infants. Hopefully, as they grow, they learn to balance a concern for themselves with a concern for others.

You can cultivate love in your inner person as you adjust your attitude to believe you aren't the most important creature in the world. God designed us to look out for others' concerns along with our own.

That balanced concern allows us to love and comes from developing the mind-set based on the value of others. Rom. 5:8 tells us that we had enough value as sinners for God to love us. Each person has an innate value that God recognizes. We need to recognize that same value.

That value doesn't come from behavior: no one can be good enough for a pure God to love him or her based on what he or she does. We tend to *like* people who are likable, who are like us, who do good things to us. Liking usually comes from traits or behavior in others.

As men, doesn't that form the basis of most of our friendships? We share some activity; perhaps we work at the same company; perhaps we play sports together; perhaps we share the same hobby. We hang with them because we like them and what they do.

But we *love* people because they're people, not because of their worthiness. People need love. We need to give love. The God of love imbeds that love in our character. According to Jesus in Matt. 5:43-48, that's love:

You have heard that it was said, "Love your neighbor and hate your enemy." But I tell you: Love your enemies and pray for those who persecute you, that you may be sons of your Father in heaven. He causes his sun to rise on the evil and the good, and sends rain on the righteous and the unrighteous. If you love those who love you, what reward will you get? Are not even the tax collectors doing that? And if you greet only your brothers, what are you doing more than others? Do not even pagans do that? Be perfect, therefore, as your heavenly Father is perfect.

Jesus strongly connected our becoming children of God and our loving the unlovely. The unlovely includes those who bring us distress. That means we take concrete action—like praying—on their behalf. Why? Because that's God's character, and He wants His children to be like Him.

We can consciously cultivate an awareness of the innate value that all people have. The first step in that cultivation process involves weeding. Certain attitudes and actions can choke out the growth of love, so we need to weed them out.

WEED OUT

Two weeds work against developing love: the weed of selfishness and the weed of selective love.

Selfishness

First of all, let's recognize that preoccupation with self is natural. We'll never eliminate our concern for ourselves; God gave it as a means of self-protection. But we need to weed out that attitude's domination of us. According to Phil. 2:3-8, when we balance our innate concern for ourselves with a care for others, we weed out selfishness.

Do nothing out of selfish ambition or vain conceit, but in humility consider others better than yourselves. Each of you should look *not only* to his own interests, but *also* to the interests of others. Your attitude should be the same as that of Christ Jesus: Who, being in very nature God, did not consider equality with God something to be grasped, but made himself nothing, taking the very nature of a servant, being made in human likeness. And being found in appearance as a man, he humbled himself and became obedient to death —even death on a cross! (emphasis added).

How do we overcome our innate selfishness? By adding an active concern for others. Loving others doesn't mean we completely ignore our own valid needs and interests. But we develop a balance. We look after our interests. We *also* look after the interests of others. We escape the trap of self-centeredness.

Jesus did that in the passage above. When He lives in us, He reveals His character in and through us. We become loving, because we're children of God. We balance our needs with those of others. We're not being exclusively concerned with either others or self. We can so easily get out of balance.

Some people are so absorbed with themselves that they never even see the neediness of others. They dedicate themselves to "looking out for Number 1." We don't need to identify Number 1, do we? Why do men do such a good job here? Self-absorption is even a problem for some churches that focus almost entirely on meeting the needs of its members. One large church in the Northwest has no budget for missions whatsoever. The church proclaims, "Our mission field is our city." That both ignores others and caters to its innate self-interest.

Churches caught up in the health-and-wealth "gospel" also fit into this category. I recently viewed a television preacher who repeatedly emphasized, "I want it all." He made it clear that he didn't want all of godliness but rather the stuff of life that brings "pleasure."

But others sacrifice too much. They ignore their own valid needs out of a misbegotten idea of love. "If it gives me pleasure, it must be wrong." They sacrifice, but they sacrifice genuine needs and soon burn out. Some churches focus on this side of the coin to the exclusion of the other and end up wearing their people out.

Our needs are important. True needs are needs. They're non-negotiable. We must look after them, but they alone can't drive our lives. We weed out selfishness by adding a concern for others to our concern for ourselves. Others have needs, too, some that only we can satisfy.

As you actively build concern for others, as you look for concrete ways to express your love, you then weed out the innate selfishness that men tend to battle. As God develops His character in you, you become like Him: loving in all you do.

Partial Love

One of the most hindering weeds to developing love as a deep-down character trait is partial success. We see some progress in becoming more loving and take justifiable pride in it. We love some people deeply, even though we don't love all people. Or we love many people, even though we don't love them deeply.

But that partial growth in being more loving can make us think we've arrived. We have some genuine love and act loving sometimes, and we think that "sometimes" is enough. But that love is only partial.

Partial isn't enough. This surface love can sidetrack us from getting love deep down into our character. We love in part when we love those who are easy to love, who love us. We justify not loving others by rationalizing that they don't deserve love or that we do love some people. That's not love. The character trait of genuine love extends to all people.

A visiting admiral talked to the enlisted men on a Navy ship and asked one, "What would you do if another sailor fell overboard?"

He promptly replied, "I'd raise the alarm and toss him a life preserver, sir."

The admiral then asked, "What would you do if it were an officer?"

At this, the sailor paused and thought before replying, "Which one, sir?"

Men tend to love those who are like themselves, but when God's love fills our being, we have a godly compassion for all people—not just those we like and identify with. We gain that compassion when we recognize the innate, God-given value that every person has.

God loved us while we were still sinners. We need to value people the way God does. Then we can feel some of their pain, we can begin to identify with them through our shared brokenness. Rom. 12:15 is the pattern. "Rejoice with those who rejoice; mourn with those who mourn."

How do you weed out selective love? Begin the process by thinking and acting toward all people as you know God would. Value each person equally, as God does. And act in love toward them all.

Don't look on others as your audience. Draw out their opinions and seek to discover how God works in them. It's important to get beneath the surface of trivial conversation about how your favorite team is performing, the weather, or the sale at the sporting goods store. Work on doing this with everyone. Why? Because love can't be selective but must be given fully to all, just as God does.

NURTURE THE FRUIT OF LOVE

Just as we eliminate anything that works against godly love, so must we deliberately nurture that which enhances love. First we need to nurture the attitude that places a high value on loving others consistently.

The Value of Love

Love provides a focal point for the Christian life, where all aspects of faith come together. All that we are and do flows from love. Jesus made that clear in Matt. 22:37-40, when someone asked about the greatest commandment.

Love the Lord your God with all your heart and with all your soul and with all your mind. This is the first and greatest commandment. And the second is like it: "Love your neighbor as yourself." All the Law and the Prophets hang on these two commandments.

Jesus went beyond the original question about the greatest commandment, because He couldn't separate the second-greatest commandment from the first. Jesus taught that all the important changes depend on loving God and loving others.

When we allow God's character to shape ours, then we become the person God designed us to be. We express God. All that we are should flow from the love of God within us. Paul made that clear in Gal. 5:6—"In Christ Jesus neither circumcision nor uncircumcision has any value. The only thing that counts is *faith expressing itself through love"* (emphasis added).

What we do, by itself, has no value in pleasing God. That threatens those of us men who think that if we just do the right things we'll be OK. Trying to express love is much more difficult. For most of us, loving isn't natural.

We nurture love by realizing its centrality, so we can please God, so we can live the Christian life, and so we can develop God's character. We value love more than pleasing ourselves. We consciously think, *How can I best express the love of God in this situation?* To achieve that, we must nurture our awareness of God's presence in us, because love flows from His character.

God's Love in Us

The only way we can love from our character is when God is in us. Some people, by their natures, love more easily than others. But many of us don't love as we should. We "look out for Number 1," and others take a distant second place—until God gives us love, as revealed in Rom. 5:5—"Hope does not disappoint us, because God has *poured out his love into our hearts* by the Holy Spirit, whom he has given us" (emphasis added).

The Christian character trait of love doesn't come from our own natural, inborn ability to love. If so, many of us could never love. But God gives us part of His character: the ability to love. According to 1 John 4:16, when God lives in us, love lives in us. "We know and rely on the love God has for us. *God is love.* Whoever lives in love lives in God, and God in him" (emphasis added).

The very essence of God is love. God can't act unlovingly— that would violate His nature. And if that loving God lives within us, then love lives within us. That's made more clear in 1 John 3:1-2:

> How great is the love the Father has *lavished* on us, that we should be called children of God! And that is what we are! The reason the world does not know us is that it did not know him. Dear friends, now we are children of God, and what we will be has not yet been made known. But we

know that when he appears, we shall *be like him,* for we shall see him as he is (emphasis added).

God has already lavished love on us. Present perfect tense—it's already been done. He gave us the tremendous privilege of being his children. Whatever this last verse says about our spiritual bodies, our roles and duties in heaven, we do know that we shall be like Him.

The love God has poured into us will reach its completion in heaven, but that love starts on earth. As soon as Christ comes to live within us, we take on His character trait of love. And since love flows out of God by nature, when we allow God to express himself in us, then we'll see love flowing out of our lives—a fruit of who's within us.

Even if envy, discord, selfishness, hatred, and anger fill our natural character, God can change all that. The love of God will transform a believer. When God changes the nature of our "tree," we bear fruit reflective of our new nature.

We don't love on our own; we let God love through us. And we gradually don't just *act* lovingly—we *become* more loving deep down. Love becomes imbedded in our lives as a fruit of the Spirit—fruit that's ripe, mature, and pleasing to all around it. But that takes action on our part.

Training to Love Through Repeated Action

Many of us have played sports, and we've learned that an athlete trains by doing *the proper thing* over and over until it becomes a habit. Practice doesn't make *perfect.* Practice only makes *permanent* whatever we practice. In 1 Tim. 4:7 the apostle Paul told his protégé Timothy to "train yourself to be godly." The central issue in being godly is to be loving, so we need to train ourselves to love. How?

In any situation, before we act we need to ask, *According to God, what's the most loving thing to do? What can I do to make life better for this person, to help him or her grow spiritually?*

We begin with having God's love within, desiring it to permeate our character, then acting out loving behavior as we implant the trait.

Sometimes, regarding a person whom we really struggle to love, we can ask, *How can I best express God's love to this person?* We may honestly realize we struggle with loving the person, but we couple that struggle with a greater desire to channel God's love to him or her through us.

For those we have a hard time even *wanting* to love, that can help. We realize that God wants us to love the person, and we can't on our own. But we can act as a channel for God's love to that person.

Once we determine the most loving act, we act—in love, not from fickle feelings but from a deep-down desire for the person's best. And we continue to act in love.

The Cost of Love

The choice to act in love will often carry a cost. Guys, love often demands a sacrifice. Time, finances, and pride are just a few of the expenses of love. We need to strike a balance in loving people and meeting their needs, with loving ourselves and meeting our needs. We continually battle to find equilibrium between our needs and others' needs.

The manly character trait of love means we choose not only to look after our own needs but also to escape the trap of self and to have compassion and action for others as well.

As you continue the process of training yourself in love, love gets deeper down into your character. The foreign acts of love become less so. You will find it easier to define the loving act. You will act in love more easily.

As love gets more deeply imbedded into your character, the Holy Spirit expresses more of His fruit in your life. That fruit becomes mature and pleasing and beneficial to others.

Jesus said in John 13:35, "By this all men will know you are my disciples, if you love one another." In the first century that happened. A non-Christian historian of that era said of those Christians, "Behold how they love one another." They developed the Christian character trait of love deep down into their persons. We men today can do the same. Try to imagine Christian men as having a reputation in our culture as men strong enough to sacrifice for others. Wouldn't that be awesome?

When you have God's inner compassion for others, then your behavior will flow from your heart of love. You'll have integrity and will be the same person on the outside as you are on the inside. Your behavior will match your attitude of love. That's the lesson of 1 John 3:16-18:

> This is how we know what love is: Jesus Christ laid down his life for us. And we ought to lay down our lives for our brothers. If anyone has material possessions and sees his brother in need but has no pity on him, how can the love of God be in him? Dear children, let us not love with words or tongue but with actions and in truth.

Ouch! If we see a person in need, have the means to meet that need, and do nothing, then we don't possess the love of God. Since God is love, then does God himself live in us? John teaches that since God is a God of love, then His children will reflect His love in concrete actions to help others.

If we don't help people, then others can conclude that the God of love isn't within us. Remember Jesus' statement of how we see the inner reality by the outer fruit? What does a lack of loving fruit say about our inner character?

Whatever material possessions we have, whether time, money, skill, a car, a house, we need to use them in a balanced way to both meet our own valid needs and the valid needs of others. Christians tend to do that naturally when God lives within.

Examples of Love in Action

We had an interesting week some time ago at our church as our people lived out love. One of our members, Marci, had been the victim of rape and was scheduled to testify in court. The trauma of publicly recounting her violation was made worse by the presence in court of the perpetrator, a family friend. She said later she got through the situation all right since she saw an angel sitting in the courtroom.

I do believe in angels, but I wondered if she might be losing touch with reality—until she explained the "angel" was a 230-pound man from the church who took the day off to attend court with her.

Another member, Joe, had his compact truck break down 50 miles from home. Mike took Saturday off to tow it back with his full-size truck. Tom and Sam repaired it Sunday afternoon so Joe could drive to work on Monday. What do you call these two cases? Normal Christian men. Men living out God's character trait of love.

Granted, we can fake loving behavior for a while. But over time, glaring weaknesses will appear if the behavior doesn't come from inner character. We can't have deep-seated consistency in loving behavior until God himself rebuilds our character with His love. Our actions change as God imbeds His love in our character.

COMMIT TO GROW IN LOVE

When God and His love imbed themselves at the core of your character, you will treat people differently. You will think differently about yourself. Your relationship with God will deepen.

As you cultivate the presence of the Holy Spirit in your life, as you follow Him every moment of every day, as you allow love to be the foundation for your new character in Christ, then you will see some major changes in your identity. Love becomes part of your nature, and people see it in your behavior.

Granted, love isn't a natural trait for most of us men. But working with God allows us to develop His love deeply into our character. Work through the following questions as part of your process of nurturing love.

BECOMING MORE MANLY

1. Why do you think the "Have It Your Way" marketing strategies work so well? Are you susceptible to those strategies?

2. Have you seen yourself being selfish, as mentioned in Phil. 2:21—"Everyone looks out for his own interests, not those of Jesus Christ"? Think of one specific example. How did that make you feel about yourself?

3. What is your working definition of love? Is it closer to the Bible's definition or to the world's?

4. On a scale of 1 to 5, with 1 representing "I have no love" and 5 representing "I most often respond with love," what would be your score? What would you like it to be?

5. The book ties in behavior to true love. Do you believe this is true? Why or why not? Support your answer with scripture.

6. In 1 Cor. 13 there are several descriptions of love. Which is most difficult for you to express?

7. Give an example of the fine line of doing something out of love for others, and looking out for your own interests.

8. Jesus was the same on the inside as the outside in the area of love. What was His secret, and how can we be more like Him?

9. In 1 John 3:18 we are told to love not with words but with actions. How are you doing in this area, and what could you do this week to improve?

10. List three things God has done this month to show His love for you. How does His love make you feel?

11. What weeds threaten to choke out the love in your life? What can you do to pull these weeds?

12. With your small group, spouse, or a close friend, talk over one decision you have made to allow love to grow in your life. How can they help you in this? Be specific.

2
SMILING THROUGH THE TEARS

THE MANLY TRAIT OF JOY

The fruit of the Spirit is . . . joy.
Galatians 5:22

WHILE WORKING AT HIS FIRST JOB as a landscape contractor, George had to remove a large oak stump from a farmer's field. He also was using dynamite for the first time. With the farmer watching, George tried to hide his nervousness by carefully calculating the size of the stump, the proper amount of dynamite, and where to place it.

Finally he and the farmer moved to the detonator behind his pickup truck. With a silent prayer, George plunged the detonator. The stump gracefully rose through the air and then crashed onto the cab of the truck. George gazed in despair at the ruined cab, but the farmer was all admiration.

"Son, with a little more practice, those stumps will land in the bed of the truck every time!"

When we face adversity, we choose how to respond. Do we look at the crushed cab and give in to despair, depression, and discouragement? Or do we see how close to the bed we came and express joy and optimism? The choice comes from the Christian character trait of joy.

All men face adversity—on the job, in our marriages, with the neighbors and their barking dog. And that adversity tends to drag us down. We get tired of the constant battles. We get discouraged by the repeated defeats.

God wants to instill in us His own character trait of joy, which doesn't depend upon the situation. God is joy. For us, joy is a realistic optimism that believes God's presence within us exceeds any difficulties that threaten to overwhelm us.

The Bible consistently contrasts joy with sorrow, grief, despair, and discouragement. We can choose those as our responses to the afflictions of life. Either we're driven to despair by difficulties, or with God we transcend them. Cultivating the presence of God provides the only way to transcend tribulation.

Without denying the pain, we can smile through the tears of life. That's what God wants to implant within our character—the trait of joy. But joy isn't the absence of affliction. Ironically, joy comes only as we realize the difficulty of life. Hardship is normal.

Disappointment and discouragement come when we don't realize our hopes. If we have the attitude that life should be fair, we get depressed when it isn't. If we believe it's our right to have a high-paying, satisfying job, or if we believe those we love should treat us with full consideration, then we're targets for discouragement and will rarely find joy.

If we want joy to be planted deep in our lives, we must have the clear understanding that it doesn't come from ease. In fact, the natural condition of life is hardship.

OUR NATURAL TENDENCY: DIFFICULTY BRINGS PAIN

In John 16:33 Jesus gave a promise about life, one seldom repeated by us: "I have told you these things, so that in me you may have peace. In this world *you will have trouble.* But take heart! I have overcome the world" (emphasis added).

We hear the last part, that Jesus has overcome the world. But do we hear many sermons on Jesus' promise on the reality of tribulation? Television proclaims prosperity, health, and having all you want. But the Bible promises that God's people go through hard times.

Read the faith chapter, Heb. 11. "Faith's hall of fame" includes people who were tortured, beaten, imprisoned, stoned, cut in two, and forced to wander through the wilderness in rags. Their faith in God brought on those difficulties.

Some hard times just come from living in a world filled with pain and trouble. But some troubles directly result from following God. Following God doesn't grant us a reprieve from pain—we'll sometimes get more.

The next two sections will go into great depth establishing that difficulties are part of life and that godly people respond to these with various forms of pain. Why spend so much time on this? Because many leaders teach today that we "create our own reality," that we can speak prosperity, ease, and health, and receive them, that if we believe, life will be easy. Some teach that sickness, depression, and worry are signs of weak faith.

When we expect only good things to come our way, and when the reality of life doesn't match up, disappointment with God often follows. We think that God didn't do His part. The Bible makes it clear that difficulties are part of life and that Christians get depressed. It teaches that joy doesn't come from an easy life but from something deeper.

We'll examine five areas of difficulty that we all face, along with three typical and unhealthy reactions to difficulties. Our goal is to learn how to deal with these problems of life through the character trait of joy.

AREAS OF DIFFICULTY

Let's look just at the life of David. Remember: David was a man after God's own heart. God wanted to bless him and overwhelmingly did.

But did God remove difficulty from David's life to increase his joy? Not at all. David experienced great suffering. Each adversity that David faced represents an area in which you and I struggle. The first source of trouble deals with our physical bodies.

Physical Difficulties

Listen to David's pain in Ps. 31:10: "My life is consumed by anguish and my years by groaning; my strength fails because of my affliction, and my bones grow weak."

David went through physical distress. Whether from illness, accident, or unresolved guilt, physical suffering is common in life. I'm discovering that it's much more common at 56 than at 23. Minor sprains take months to heal. Our bodies age and decay; just as we enjoy our humanity, we also suffer from it. That was reality for David; that is reality for us. Our relationships also bring grief.

Friction with People

Some wit or half-wit proclaimed, "I like life—it's people I hate." We all struggle with people, so did David in Ps. 31:11-13:

> Because of all my enemies, I am the utter contempt of my neighbors; I am a dread to my friends—those who see me on the street flee from me. I am forgotten by them as if I were dead; I have become like broken pottery. For I hear the slander of many; there is terror on every side; they conspire against me and plot to take my life.

Our imperfection causes grief to others. We're not always understanding, kind, and forgiving. Neither are others. Their imperfections cause grief for us. Science defines friction as two uneven surfaces that rub against one another, producing heat. That sounds like a normal relationship!

Even the best relationships go through struggles, and not all relationships are the best. More tribulations result from sins we don't deal with.

Unrepented-of Sin

We men often find it difficult to acknowledge our mistakes. Since so much of our self-worth comes from our accomplishments, we tend to resist saying we failed. When we fail to acknowledge our sin, that failure itself brings difficulties. Those complications can sometimes exceed the consequences of our original sin. That's what David found in Ps. 38:3-8:

> Because of your wrath there is no health in my body; my bones have no soundness because of my sin. My guilt has overwhelmed me like a burden too heavy to bear. My wounds fester and are loathsome because of my sinful folly. I am bowed down and brought very low; all day long I go about mourning. My back is filled with searing pain; there is no health in my body. I am feeble and utterly crushed; I groan in anguish of heart.

Sound familiar? Complications of unrepentant sin range from overwhelming guilt to depression to physical infirmity. Financial problems also increase the pain of life.

Economic Adversity

Jesus promised that we would always have the poor. Don't look now, but that promise is proven all the time as we bounce from economic recession to abundance. By the summer of 1994, one-third of the homes in our valley went back to the bank or mortgage company. Bill Clinton ran on the slogan "It's the economy, stupid," won the election, and presided over the .com boom, which in turn went bust.

Homelessness spirals. The gap between the upper and lower economic classes widens. Many men are unemployed or underemployed. Many in poverty work full time, but their wages aren't enough to live on. This greatly impacts men, who are often the primary wage-earners and whose self-esteem is built on providing for their families.

This isn't new, according to David in Ps. 40:17—"I am poor and needy; may the Lord think of me. You are my help and my deliverer; O my God, do not delay."

At times David had tremendous wealth; at other times he was poor. David's psalms reveal his grief at the abuse of the poor, at the problems poverty brings. The final example is confronting the specter of death.

Death

We all face death, for ourselves and those we love. Remember, men, how we once rejoiced in our youthful years of invincibility and physicality? But that vigor fades, and eventually we realize we're not exempt. Friends and family are unfairly taken from us, and we struggle as David did in Ps. 6:5—"No one remembers you when he is dead. Who praises you from the grave?"

Considering death, we wonder at life's fairness, its meaning. We don't want to relax the grip on life.

These problems are normal, normal in the sense that we should expect them, that we shouldn't be surprised when they happen. David, a man after God's own heart, wasn't protected from the presence of problems. We won't be either.

But how did David respond? Like a superman, always happy and cheerful? Or did these problems eat at him, attacking his faith in God? Did he question the fairness of life? Examining David's responses, we discover that we have much in common with this man.

UNHEALTHFUL REACTIONS TO DIFFICULTIES

Being a typical human, David suffered with his struggles. Life's burdens weren't easy to him. Let's look at three of his responses.

Anxiety

We worry about how difficulties will impact our future. David went through that in Psalm 6:6. "I am worn out by groaning; all night long I flood my bed with weeping and drench my couch with tears."

Have you ever spent the night tossing and turning in bed, your mind going 100 miles per hour, chewing on a problem? You can't tell anyone—your wife, friends, or family. All you sense is fear, the unknown, and loss. I've spent more than one sleepless night because of a problem in the church, a personal issue, or the problems of a friend. Concern and worry seem to possess us. We feel helpless, out of control.

We feel responsible for the situation, and anxiety multiplies our pain. Problems also bring a physical impact.

Physical Problems

God created us with three parts: soul, spirit, and body. Those three parts make up one person; what affects one part will affect the other parts. Doctors have long said up to 75 percent of all illness originates in the mind. Our physical health is often tied to the health of our minds and our emotions.

Many people react to stress with physical illness. David experienced that also, as seen in the next verse, Ps. 6:7—"My eyes grow weak with sorrow; they fail because of all my foes."

We may become listless, we may get the flu and colds with greater frequency and regularity. Why? Because our bodies are linked to our minds and emotions.

Depression

We are shown in Ps. 31:9-10 how some respond to tribulation with depression.

Be merciful to me, O LORD, for I am in distress; my eyes grow weak with sorrow, my soul and my body with grief. My life is consumed by anguish and my years by groaning; my strength fails because of my affliction, and my bones grow weak.

When we feel overpowered by our difficulties, depression often results. We can't get energy to do anything. Emotionally, we want to give up. Despair takes over. Sorrow is a close friend, but not a good one. When we see the proverbial light at the end of the tunnel, we know it's just an onrushing train.

A non-Christian in this condition must have penned the phrase "Life is tough—then you die." We look at life through gray-colored glasses. We expect the worst, and then we receive it. Our shoulders droop. Our voices lower. Our eyes look down. We wear frowns.

All we see is the crushed cab, the huge bill to repair it, the days we won't have the truck for work, the laughingstock we'll be to the community.

Initial responses of anxiety, sickness, and depression are typical, for David and for us. Don't feel guilty about them, as if you're a spiritual failure. Your long-term response comes from how your character interacts with your perception of life. Is life your friend? Your foe? And most important, what makes life good or bad? This is where the Christian character trait of optimism, or joy, comes in.

THE MANLY CHARACTER TRAIT OF JOY

We frequently confuse happiness and joy. Webster does, basically calling joy the emotion we feel when things go our way. But the Christian character trait of joy comes from the center of our being and is independent of life's difficulties. A joyful character produces an optimistic outlook on life. We'll use the two terms "joy" and "optimism" somewhat interchangeably.

JOY DEFINED

Joy doesn't come from the external circumstances. That's *happiness*, which results from what's *happening*. The words "happiness" and "happening" go together. Typically, when good things happen, we're happy. When bad things happen, we're not happy.

A sugar package found in a restaurant said, "An optimist is someone who tells you to cheer up—when things are going his way."

That's not optimism but happiness. The difference is major. If our "optimism" comes from external circumstances, we'll be up when things go as we desire, and we'll be down when they don't go as we desire.

Even great spiritual victories won't bring lasting joy. Elijah learned this after his tremendous victory over the prophets of Baal in 1 Kings 18—19.

After the victory, fear and depression filled Elijah. Anxious about the consequences for his life, he was ready to die. Why? His focus was on the externals, not on the inward presence of God. Only that inward presence produces optimism.

God offers you a change of character so you can consistently have optimism and joy in your life, regardless of the difficulties. As John Sanderson says in his book *The Fruit of the Spirit*, "Joy does not depend on outer circumstances but on the reality of God."

Let me share my working definition of joy. Optimism is "believing the reasons to be excited about life exceed the reasons to get discouraged and negative."

Godly joy enables us to not merely react. We're not the puppet of problems, with our emotions moving up or down like the stock market. Optimism allows us to choose our responses. We may not always be happy, but we can always be joyful and optimistic. As we analyze the source of joy, we'll see the truth of that.

WHERE JOY IS FOUND

If happiness comes from what happens, then joy and enthusiasm come from deep down. We'll look at two specific sources of joy, the presence of God within the deepest recesses of our lives, and how God works for our good in trials.

Joy through the Presence of God

Many verses link joy and the presence of God in our lives.

For further study, examine passages such as Acts 16:34; Rom. 14:17; 1 Thess. 1:6. For now, let's just look at Ps. 16:8-11—

> I have set the LORD always before me. Because he is at my right hand, I will not be shaken. Therefore my heart is glad and my tongue rejoices; my body will also rest secure, because you will not abandon me to the grave, nor will you let your Holy One see decay. You have made known to me the path of life; *you will fill me with joy in your presence*, with eternal pleasures at your right hand (emphasis added).

Look at that last sentence. We gain the Christian character trait of joy from the presence of God. His presence assures us that the reasons to be excited about life are greater than the reasons to get discouraged and negative.

Real reasons to get discouraged exist, as David experienced. But problems aren't the whole story. A Christian living in perpetual gloom is somewhat like reading a murder mystery until the key characters are done away with. Then we put the book down, discouraged that the murder hasn't been solved. But it's not over. We haven't read the finish.

Christians sometimes remember the passage on tribulation, John 16:33, that in this world we will have trouble. We whimper a weak "Amen." But we quit reading too soon! Jesus finished by saying, "But take heart! I have overcome the world."

The same Jesus who overcame the world lives in us. We don't have to be dragged down by negativity. Nor do we retreat to a rose-colored-glasses view of reality, ignoring pain. We counter real problems with the overcoming presence of God in our hearts.

The awesomeness of God's presence overbalances the tendency to get discouraged. We need to grab onto this principle, to think about it at least once per second until it's imbedded in our minds, to realize that the majestic, awesome, transcendent Creator of everything lives within us.

Joy then builds into a character trait. By continually repeating that thought until it becomes a habit, joy gets deep down. That trait establishes our outlooks on life as optimistic, positive, and enthusiastic.

If we can't get excited about the concept of God living within us, then we get excited about the wrong things. If God's presence isn't enough to overcome any problem, then our view of God is much too puny.

When looking at our problems heightens our negativity, we balance that by thinking about the God who lives within. That's enthusiasm.

Enthusiasm comes from a compound Greek word. *En* means "in," *theos* means "God." We have enthusiasm when we realize that we're *in God*. Enthusiasm doesn't exist because the circumstances of life go well. Much of the time, things don't go well.

But optimism grows within us as a character trait, when we're convinced God is in us. To paraphrase an old line, "God's in my life, and all's right with the world."

This is perspective. If we primarily focus on the bad in life, if we suspect that the future will only bring more pain, then depression and discouragement are inescapable. Problems grow in both number and magnitude until they become overwhelming.

But if we primarily focus on God's presence, then the future holds little fear. Optimism and joy are normal responses. We neither ignore nor are overwhelmed with life's problems.

With a high view of God's love and power, then His presence becomes more important than the presence of problems. No circumstance can overshadow that.

Some problems may discourage us for a short time. Temporary depression afflicted both David and Elijah. But depression doesn't have to become a permanent part of our lives—not when balanced with the powerful and exuberant presence of the Creator.

We find joy through the presence of God in our lives. That's how we find joy in the worst of our troubles.

Joy in the Midst of Trials

Morrie Brooks came to Christ late in life. Raised as a Jew with an awareness of spiritual matters, he said that this awareness rarely impacted how he lived. His ambition drove him to the vice-presidency of a major corporation, with debris strewn along the way, including fractured relationships with his wife and children.

Shortly before Morrie's retirement, cancer and a bad heart raced one another to end his life. But God used a gently persistent hospital chaplain and a midnight vision to bring him to Christ. He left the hospital with the cancer removed, his heart repaired, and a new life begun.

During the next five years an inquiring, hungry heart provided the impetus to relational healing and spiritual growth. Then the cancer returned to stay. In his home on October 31, Morrie went home to be with the God he came to know and love. A comment that day by his son Nate struck home: "I've always hated Halloween—it's Satan's day. But I'm going to look at Halloween differently now. My dad beat Satan at his own game, on his day."

Did Morrie's death bring sorrow? Obviously. His family and friends lost someone they loved. But God's presence added joy to the anguish. Joy can be found in the worst of trials. Happiness won't be, since it comes from what's happening.

Many bad things happen. But we can always have joy, because God is always within us. That's made clear in James 1:2-4: "Consider it pure joy, my brothers, whenever you face trials of many kinds, because you know that the testing of your faith develops perseverance. Perseverance must finish its work so that you may be mature and complete, not lacking anything."

That goes against our grain. Consider it *pure joy* when the storms of life come? Some joy, maybe. Pure joy, no way. Are we excited at trials because we're masochistic, because we love to feel pain? Not at all.

We can experience joy because we know that God will use pain to perfect us, to make us all we can be. How does that work?

Michelangelo was asked how he created the masterpiece *David*. He responded, "I merely got a piece of marble and chiseled away anything that didn't look like David."

I'm sure that if the marble had a nervous system, the pain level would have been intense as parts of its being were pounded off. But look at the result.

Think back on the easy, good times, the kind we get happy about. Did that happiness cause us to dig deeply into the meaning of life, of just who we were? Did happiness cause us to refine ourselves to eliminate any impurities? Or did we just savor those times and float along downstream?

Think back also on some of the more difficult times. Didn't that pain reveal what within us caused the situation? Didn't that pain build a desire to eliminate what caused the grief? The trials of life force us to search, meditate, and change.

How do men grow into Christian masculinity? How does God implant joy in us? By working through difficulties. By discovering what "doesn't look like David" in our persons and allowing God to chisel that away.

By developing endurance rather than quitting at the first sign of hardship, by being committed to the process of how God works in us, we allow the crises of life to motivate us to eliminate anything that shouldn't be there.

Joy comes from not being caught up in the present pain but from seeing the eventual result. Satan will attempt to use these events to bring discouragement and depression. God will use those same events to bring maturity and completion. What will bring more joy than to accomplish the opposite of what Satan is trying to do?

We beat Satan at his own game when we turn events that normally bring pain into joy. When we look at the long term instead of just the short term, we can have the character trait of joy through difficulties.

In a brief search, I discovered nine passages that mention joy and difficulties together. Those difficulties include death, sickness, friction with people, and poverty. Coincidence? I think not. This connection of joy and problems confuses most non-Christians. They find it hard to smile through the tears of life.

While just in his 30s, Sam died unexpectedly of a heart attack, leaving behind a wife and several young children. The owner of the apartment building Sam managed was a member of our church and asked me to conduct the funeral service. Neither Sam nor his family or friends had any background of faith or church involvement, which set the mood for the service.

You can't "preach someone into heaven," but at a funeral I try to focus on reasons to celebrate the life of the person. I bring out his or her good points and give the people a chance to share precious memories. Despite that, gloom hung over the crowd like a dark cloud. They couldn't begin to smile through their tears. All they could see was pain, loss, and no hope.

We Christians face the same dark clouds of life. We cry. We grieve. We get depressed and discouraged. We're tempted to give up. But difficulties don't defeat us. Pain doesn't put us down for the count. We know there's more to the story. We have hope.

Because we know the end of the story, we can smile through the tears. We can enjoy life, even when life brings pain. Some will accuse us of "pretending" or ignoring reality. Actually, we know reality better than others. Others ignore the reality of God working in the worst of times to bring the best, in time.

Non-Christians struggle to comprehend that. They don't understand the dynamic, because they don't have the presence who can transform trouble. We can have joy in the midst of troubles, because we have God in us to work for good with the worst of situations.

CULTIVATING THE MANLY TRAIT OF JOY

As a fruit of the Spirit, joy develops over time. The first step in cultivation eliminates qualities that work against joy. The most dangerous weed in the garden of joy is negativity, when we expect bad experiences to come and overwhelm us. Pessimism destroys optimism unless we weed it out.

WEED OUT NEGATIVITY

Phil. 4:4 calls us to rejoice always. Joy grows into a character trait when we change our thoughts, as found in Phil. 4:8—"Brothers, whatever is true, whatever is noble, whatever is right, whatever is pure, whatever is lovely, whatever is admirable—if anything is excellent or praiseworthy—think about such things."

Is looking for the bad noble? Is focusing just on our problems lovely? Is complaining about our situation praiseworthy? Godly joy comes from our thoughts about life. When problems fill our thoughts, we don't have room to rejoice over the presence of God.

How do we drive out negative thoughts? By replacing them with positive ones. If we tell ourselves, *Don't think negatively,* all we think of is the negative. The classic challenge not to think of pink elephants makes us think of them.

Negative thoughts are the same. To eliminate the thoughts that bring depression and discouragement, we replace them with other thoughts—thoughts that will build on the presence of God in our lives, that will build joy into our deep-down character.

NURTURE THE FRUIT OF JOY

We eliminate the destructive thoughts and build joy when we find reasons to rejoice, instead of reasons to get down. In the same way Morrie's son Nate dealt with his grief by realizing that his dad beat Satan on his own day, by reminding himself that on this day his father overcame death with victory.

In studying verses on joy, I was amazed by what I didn't find. Not a single verse told *how* to rejoice—just to do it. How do we eliminate those poisonous, negative thoughts? By finding a reason to rejoice, and then rejoicing. Joy is a natural response when we remind ourselves of several truths. Let me share three reasons to rejoice, ways we can nurture optimism.

Focus on God's Presence

When we think of how the awesome God lives in us, we can get excited. As we think of what He's done to show His love for us, we can get enthusiastic. Thinking of how in the worst of times God was there hugging us closely causes us to celebrate. We build joy into a deep-down trait as we train ourselves to focus on His presence.

An old story tells of a new believer who read the verse telling us to "pray at all times." Not having already been taught that prayer is a certain time alone with God, he pondered how to pray while driving, at work, and in conversations. He finally decided to begin each day with his first waking thought, *Dear God . . .* and to end his day with the last thought before falling asleep, *In Jesus' name. Amen.*

He learned what it means to live in the presence of God!

Remember Ps. 16:11—"You will fill me with joy in your presence." That means as we cultivate an awareness of God's continual presence with us, we cultivate the trait of joy. Why?

Can you think of anything more exciting than always being with the Creator of the universe? Imagine the living person you most admire. Wouldn't you be thrilled to spend several hours with him or her, asking any question you desired, learning from him or her, or just quietly being with the person, knowing that he or she truly wanted to spend some time with you?

For a Christian, nobody should excite us like God. Just being with God is far better than the worst situation is bad. As we build on that, we build joy. We've found a reason to rejoice despite the circumstances. Another step in nurturing joy is to remind ourselves of the victory that God guarantees us in the worst problems.

Remind Ourselves of Eventual Victory

We mentioned John 16:33 earlier, in which Jesus made two promises—first, that as long as we walk this earth, we'll have trouble; and second, that we can take heart because Jesus has overcome the world.

We need to be cautious here. Jesus doesn't free us *from* problems but *through* them. That is, He doesn't eliminate them. Rather, He gives us the power not to get dragged down and be overwhelmed by them.

We also claim the ultimate victory. Despite all of Satan's attempts to use circumstances to draw us away from God, we have the power to conquer Satan's grasp on death and reach heaven. This truth brought joy to Morrie's family at his death. Satan had won a skirmish, but Morrie had won the war.

An effective tool at nurturing joy is to think of the difficult situations out of which God brought victory. If we see defeat, we experience discouragement. If we see victory, we experience joy. The choice is ours: to nurture memories of defeat or victory. Joy grows as we nurture memories of victory.

Another step in nurturing joy is to remember how God works for our spiritual growth in the worst of times.

Remind Ourselves of Growth Opportunities

Most of us are familiar with Rom. 8:28, the promise that God will work for good in all things. Not all things are good; evil abounds and touches the lives of Christians. Obviously, we don't establish the false belief that a godly life eliminates pain. But in the midst of evil, God continues to effectively work for good.

One specific way He does that is found in James 1:2-4. We briefly examined this earlier in the chapter; let's review it as a source of joy.

> Consider it pure joy, my brothers, whenever you face trials of many kinds, because you know that the testing of your faith develops perseverance. Perseverance must finish its work so that you may be mature and complete, not lacking anything.

When life goes well, we tend to enjoy it. We think we've got life wired; we know how to do it. So we don't change; we don't dig deeper. But trials shatter our complacency. Our old methods don't work. Character weaknesses are revealed.

And we change, even if it's only our last resort. We eliminate anything that works against us. We grow closer to God. We become more grounded and stable.

This passage teaches a key formula for developing the character trait of joy. Trials come, and we rejoice because we don't see just the short-term pain but also the long-term *gain*. We think, *If God allows a trial this big, He must have some great changes in store for me!*

COMMIT TO GROW IN JOY

We smile through the tears of life by nurturing the Christian character trait of joy. Joy isn't a product of our personality structure but a product of God's presence, a realization that the awesomeness of God far exceeds the awfulness of problems. Joy is our choosing to focus on the presence of God within us.

Joy isn't a natural trait for most of us. As partners of God, we strive to develop His joy deep down into our character. Work through these following questions as part of your process of nurturing joy.

BECOMING MORE MANLY

1. Describe some difficult times you've experienced recently.

2. In what ways did you see God work for victory or growth in them? How did that make you feel?

3. What is your working definition of joy? Is it closer to the Bible's definition or to the world's?

4. On a scale of 1 to 5, with 1 representing "I have no joy" and 5 representing "I most often respond with joy," what would be your score? What would you like it to be?

5. Discuss how joy is our choice.

6. What weeds most threaten to choke out joy in your life? What can you do to pull these weeds?

7. What most enhances the sense of God's presence in your life?

8. What do you feel when you strongly sense God's presence?

9. What can you do in this next week to nurture joy?

10. With your small group, spouse, or a close friend, talk over one decision you have made to allow joy to grow in your life. How can they aid you in this? Be specific.

3
SLOWING OUR SPIRIT
THE MANLY TRAIT OF PEACE

The fruit of the Spirit is . . . peace.
Galatians 5:22

TOO MANY MEN LIVE IN A WORLD with too many tasks. Count Roy in that group. A troubleshooter for a large highway construction company, he frequently travels across much of southern California checking on job sites. Whenever a glitch arises, he gets called. Broken equipment, too many workers off sick, a bad accident—all demand his presence. The company tries to work on off-peak traffic hours, so that extends his schedule to most hours of the day.

He talked about the pace of his life with one of the guys in the men's group he infrequently met with. "I gotta admit it—I'm an adrenaline junkie. I love the pressure of having to fix things. And I like being needed. Not many guys could juggle all this. You'll never hear me complain about the money; the company treats me good. A new car every other year, but at 60,000 miles a year, they need to do that.

"But I can't make a whole lot of my kids' games, and I miss that. I really miss getting with you guys each week. Luckily, we have a gardener to do most of the yard work, but I just love working on projects, planning something, getting my hands dirty.

"I know Pastor wants me to teach that class for seekers, but I can't commit to every week for a month. Worst of all, I don't see this letting up anytime soon. I do like living in the fast lane, but I wish it had a finish line."

The pace of life overwhelms us. We wait for "things to slow down," and they merely increase their speed. We feel like a puppet dancing on the end of a string somebody else jerks around. We have more projects than time. We get intimidated by the technological pace of life.

We probably won't slow down the pace of life on this side of the grave; too many factors are beyond our control. High housing costs force us to keep unpleasant jobs that pay well. Too many recreational and educational activities for our children drain our time. Job pressures force overtime. A complex culture conspires to suck up our time and energy. We can't easily change those forces.

But we men can slow down our spirits. We can nurture the Christian character trait of peace to bring a tranquility that transcends the tempo of our times. God wants to instill in us His own character trait of peace. But peace isn't inherent in us. We tend to go the opposite direction.

OUR NATURAL TENDENCY: WORRY

The biblical word for "worry" suggests having a divided mind. We get torn in two directions. We want to find peace through trusting God, but we also feel we need to take responsibility—to do something. We're men, and we largely build our self-worth on what we do. Worry is having two opposite concerns warring with one another. Peace isn't an option when worry over the stresses of life consumes our thoughts.

We see all the things that need to be done, how little time we have, and we worry. According to Jesus in Matt. 6:25-27, 31-34, anxiety is the opposite of finding peace through trust in God.

I tell you, do not worry about your life, what you will eat or drink; or about your body, what you will wear. Is not life more important than food, and the body more important than clothes? Look at the birds of the air; they do not sow or reap or store away in barns, and yet your heavenly Father feeds them. Are you not much more valuable than they? Who of you by worrying can add a single hour to his life? . . . So do not worry, saying, "What shall we eat?" or "What shall we drink?" or "What shall we wear?" For the pagans run after all these things, and your heavenly Father *knows that you need them.* But seek first his kingdom and his righteousness, and all these things will be given to you as well. Therefore do not worry about tomorrow, for tomorrow will worry about itself. Each day has enough trouble of its own (emphasis added).

Those issues of food, clothing, and shelter drive us to worry and steal our peace. If we focus on getting and holding onto them, anxiety consumes us. We have too much to do, too little time, too few resources. The alternative to being stressed over the stuff and pace of life is the Christian character trait of patience—tranquility, the ability to slow our spirit in the rush of life.

THE MANLY CHARACTER TRAIT OF PEACE

Peace isn't the absence of difficulty, stress, and being rushed. That life rarely exists for most men. The character trait of tranquility allows us to relax in the midst of a bustling society. The world makes frantic demands on our time, energy, and activities. We can't stop that. But we can still find peace.

Peace Defined

An art competition awarded a prize for the best expression of peace. One painting depicted a deer and fawn grazing at the skirt of a mountain meadow rimmed with pines and cedars stretching heavenward. Another showed a cat curled up in a basket, resting with all its being as only cats can do.

But first prize went to the painting of a tumultuous waterfall. Torrents rushed downward to dash themselves on the rocks below, sending spray high above. A tree branch extended just above the mist with a bird nest in a fork. Safely within sat a mother bird and two babies.

That's tranquility—the ability to relax in the most rushed circumstances. Serene surroundings don't necessarily produce peace. The absence of animosity doesn't. If peace depended on the setting, many could never find serenity.

Peace is being in harmony, allowing God to fit all the pieces of our lives together. As we cultivate the presence of the Holy Spirit deep down, He brings peace. It begins on the personal level, between an individual and God.

PERSONAL PEACE

Personal peace comes through knowing Jesus Christ intimately, when He's the passion that drives our lives. Lacking that will bring unrest and dissatisfaction. In the first page of *Confessions,* Augustine wrote, "Thou has made us for Thyself, and our heart is restless until it finds rest in Thee."

Psychologist Carl Jung echoed our central need for God: "Among all my patients in the second half of life, that is to say, over 35, there has not been one whose problem in the last resort was not that of finding a religious outlook on life."

Peace comes only from God, and a variety of problems result when God isn't at the center of our lives. The only source of secure peace is passionately knowing God. That will then connect all the pieces of our lives into one harmonious whole. Paul taught that in Rom. 5:1—"Since we have been justified through faith, we have peace with God through our Lord Jesus Christ."

Harmony with God brings a peace that will spread into all arenas of our lives. God harmonizes each aspect by bringing all things under His control. On my Honda Gold Wing motorcycle, power comes to the rear wheel through the hub. The hub at the center of the wheel receives the power and transmits it through the spokes to the rim. The wheel then moves.

Think of your life as that wheel. The hub is the center of your life, what motivates and drives you. The spokes are the specific areas, like your personality, character, and activities. The rim is the outer part of your life that shows action. If your spokes aren't firmly connected to God at the hub of your life, you won't move.

You may have action. The hub moves. The spokes may even flop around. But the rim doesn't move. Despite the activity, little is accomplished. Doesn't that sound like modern life? Bustling, busy, but with little finished. Perhaps that's not so old. Shakespeare spoke of "sound and fury, signifying nothing."

But when all the pieces of life are connected to God, there can be peace and harmony. Life may never slow down. You may not be able to escape the pace of life—but you can unify everything under Christ.

We're not torn in two directions, or even 20, all at the same time. We go in one direction with God. We evaluate all activities out of a desire to please Him. Like the bird nest above the waterfall, we rest easy during the storms of life.

Anxiety over paying the mortgage doesn't possess our thoughts: we trust in God's promise to meet our needs when we put Him first. We don't constantly fear health issues. Either we die physically, which brings us directly to the love of our life; or we live physically and serve Him here. If our health improves, we're pleased; but if it doesn't, we know that God's power is made perfect in our weakness (2 Cor. 12:9). Concern over government officials and school boards doesn't bring depression: what person can oppose what God truly wants done?

Instead of worrying or feeling rushed, we focus on pleasing Him. By relying on God, the center of our lives, all the pieces of our lives connect to one another. We have completeness. We have peace. We trust in God's love and power and yield personal responsibility for how things develop. Once we have this personal peace with God, then we can develop peace with others.

Interpersonal Peace

Interpersonal peace doesn't mean we bring in world peace and abolish war but that God brings peace between those He lives within. Paul commands that we have peace within the Church: "Aim for perfection, listen to my appeal, be of one mind, *live in peace*. And the God of love and *peace* will be with you" (2 Cor. 13:11, emphasis added).

Solving world violence exceeds both our grasp and our responsibility. Slowing down the hectic pace that drives us is likewise impossible. But within the Church we can live in peace. How?

Look at the command just before we're told to live in peace. "Be of one mind." When our minds passionately unite on the shared importance of God to us, then any differences we have take second place. Yes, we disagree on when and how Jesus is coming. Yes, we disagree on spiritual gifts. Yes, we disagree on many things. Differences between Christians are real. But our shared passion for Jesus Christ exceeds our differences. That passion unites us and binds us together in peace. Too often peace in the local church is merely something we read about.

"The church is the only army that shoots its wounded." We've all seen or experienced examples of that too-often-deserved description. I know of two separate churches that split over the color of carpeting in the fellowship hall. What's wrong? Placing personal preference above peace.

I grew up in a movement with a slogan from Augustine that sets the stage for peace in the church: "In essentials, unity. In non-essentials, liberty. In all things, charity [love]." Have we lived up to this consistently? Not as much as God would desire. But that goal provides the possibility of peace.

If we insist on our opinions, we'll battle and never have peace in our churches. But if we can unite around our shared passion for Christ, lesser issues slip into the background. Peace reigns between the brothers and sisters.

By aiming for perfection, with a common mindset that Jesus is most important, by yielding on our opinions for the mission of Christ while working diligently to win others to Him, we can then obey Paul's command to live in peace. Now let's discover some practical steps to developing both personal and interpersonal peace.

CULTIVATING THE MANLY TRAIT OF TRANQUILITY

Ron's job of supervising computer programmers required driving two and one-half hours each way, into the thick of southern California traffic. Crawling along at five miles per hour when you're late for work doesn't build tranquility. Nor does returning to a houseful of three outgoing, noisy teenagers. Add to this Ron's serving as an elder in his church and his leadership of a team formed to call on visitors, and you wouldn't assume this to be a recipe for tranquility.

But Ron is one of the most tranquil, peaceful men I know. Troubles tend to bring a smile; unruly children provoke firm but loving discipline with no angry outbursts. One of the most gracious men in the church, people are drawn to him by his serenity. How does he do it? Ron learned that developing tranquility first requires eliminating weeds that compete with the fruit of peace. We must nurture the Christian character trait of tranquility.

WEED OUT

Just as a vegetable garden needs to be weeded to eliminate plants that compete with the desired result, we need to eliminate traits in our lives that work against peace. According to Paul, the first weed to pluck out is worry.

Worry

Do not be anxious about anything, but in everything, by prayer and petition, with thanksgiving, present your requests to God. And the *peace of God,* which transcends all understanding, will guard your hearts and your minds in Christ Jesus (*Phil. 4:6-7,* emphasis added).

We achieve peace by eliminating anxiety and worry. Worry is a preoccupation with our responsibility to work out things in our lives. Prayer is the antidote. Peace develops when we pray, when we invite God to direct our lives. We don't become irresponsible—we still do our part—but we give to God the responsibility for results. That's what prayer is all about. The more we pray, the more peace we possess. We'll study this more a little later in the chapter. Next we weed out friction with people.

Friction with People

Just on our own, we can't insure great relationships with all. But we can each do our part to get along well with people. The traits listed by Paul work against the fruit of peace:

The acts of the sinful nature are obvious: sexual immorality, impurity and debauchery; idolatry and witchcraft; hatred, discord, jealousy, fits of rage, selfish ambition, dissensions, factions and envy; drunkenness, orgies, and the like (*Gal. 5:19-21*).

Those acts involve other people—using them for our purposes, not getting along with them. To the degree we allow qualities like dissension and envy, we decrease our tranquility. To the degree we work against these qualities, we increase peace. We also need to be on our guard against a counterfeit fruit called apathy.

Artificial Fruit

Some lead very tranquil, peaceful lives. They feel no stress;

they're relaxed. Why? They just don't care. They possess no passion. Whatever happens is OK. Ephesians 4:19 speaks of people who have "lost all sensitivity," who are past feeling.

That's not peace. Peace isn't giving up on the battles of life but continuing to fight the good fight with harmony and contentment. Peace isn't the absence of passion, nor is it the absence of struggle. Peace has a passion that unites a person's life in the struggles. So don't allow apathy to masquerade as peace in your life. Instead, cultivate the Christian character trait of tranquility.

NURTURE THE FRUIT OF PEACE

We build peace into a deep-seated character trait in three steps. First, we deepen our relationship with God.

Develop a Conscious Trust in God

Listen to the promise in Isa. 26:3—"You will keep him *in perfect peace* whose mind is steadfast, because he *trusts in you*" (emphasis added).

When we keep our minds firmly on the love and grace of God, when we trust in God's provision for us, then we can rest in His peace. But if we don't keep our mind solidly on God, if we allow the demands of life in the 21st century to overwhelm us, then we feel like that puppet dancing every time somebody pulls its strings.

The more we nurture continual contact with Almighty God, the more peace imbeds itself in our character. One method is to pray at all times, for all things.

Prayer

The Living Bible paraphrases Phil. 4:6-7 this way: "Don't worry about anything; instead, pray about everything. . . . If you do this you will experience God's peace, which is far more wonderful than the human mind can understand." The key to peace is prayer. Continual prayer is living in the presence of God. We may not talk, but we know He's there. We may not consciously listen, but we sense His presence.

Peace comes through exhaustive prayer, when nothing is too

big or too small to take to Him. When we think an issue is small enough to be our sole responsibility, we build anxiety. When we think an issue exceeds even God's ability to overcome, we eliminate the only solution to worry.

But as we pray at all times for all things, we can rest easy in God's ability to take care of us. The next step in promoting the trait of tranquility deals with our connection to fellow Christians.

Committing to the Local Church

In Eph. 4:3 Paul tells the church how to be the Church. Unity and peace are essential elements. "Make every effort to *keep the unity of the Spirit* through the *bond of peace*" (emphasis added).

The church isn't always peaceful. We're known for major fights over minor items, and that violates the blueprint God gives for His Church.

We can't have peace, either personally or interpersonally, until we're committed to and in harmony with the local church. We won't always agree with other members or the leadership. No church will fully meet our needs and desires. As long as people are in them, local churches will be imperfect.

But Christians are still to be actively involved in them. The Christian who won't commit to a local church is somewhat like a firefighter who won't go to the station, who won't fight fires with the other firefighters—but still strongly professes that he or she "believes in fighting fires."

Harmony provides a combined power that exceeds what we can accomplish as individuals. In a horse-pulling contest in Canada the winning horse pulled 9,000 pounds. The next finisher moved 8,000 pounds. Then they harnessed the two, expecting them to pull about 17,000 pounds. Instead, working together in harmony, they moved 30,000 pounds.

What have we *not* accomplished for God, because we won't work together in peace? What price have we paid for our independence? Could it be that Christ would have returned centuries ago if the Church had simply worked together in peace?

COMMIT TO GROW IN PEACE

God's solution for the fast pace of life is the Christian character trait of peace—an inner tranquility that transcends the situation, an ability to slow down our spirits in the midst of more demands than we can respond to. Peace puts God at the hub of our lives, allowing Him to organize the details, to be responsible for the outcome.

Peace begins with having a passion for God, valuing Him above all the other details of life. Peace grows deep in one's inner character when his or her mind steadfastly trusts in Him. The following questions can help you think deeply about how to develop peace in your life as part of your character.

BECOMING MORE MANLY

1. In your daily life, what most gives you a sense of being rushed and overwhelmed?

2. What have you done to try to change that? How effective were you?

3. What is your working definition of peace? Is it closer to the Bible's definition or to the world's?

4. On a scale of 1 to 5, with 1 representing "I have no peace" and 5 representing "I most often respond with peace," what would be your score? What would you like it to be?

5. What most keeps you from having a passion for God in your life that will build your tranquility? What can you do this week to improve?

6. What weeds most threaten to choke out joy in your life? What can you do to pull these weeds?

7. Why is prayer God's antidote to worry? How does it work?

8. Have you been a source of peace in your local church, or a source of irritation? What caused that, and how can you remedy it?

9. With your small group, spouse, or a close friend, talk over one decision you have made to allow peace to grow in your life. How can they help you in this? Be specific.

4
HANGING
IN THERE

THE MANLY TRAIT OF PATIENCE

The fruit of the Spirit is . . . patience.
Galatians 5:22

WHILE PILOTING A COMMUTER FLIGHT from Portland, Maine, to Boston, Henry Dempsey heard a strange noise coming from the rear of the small plane. Turning the controls over to his co-pilot, he went to check it out. Just as he discovered the rear door hadn't been secured before takeoff, the plane hit an air pocket, slamming Henry against the door. The door flew open, and Henry was sucked out of the open doorway toward the ocean below.

The co-pilot saw the open-door warning light and realized Henry had disappeared. He radioed in, requesting a helicopter search for that area of the ocean.

After the plane landed, they found Henry—but not floating in the ocean beneath the flight path. Almost miraculously, he had grabbed onto the outside ladder and held on as the plane descended from 4,000 feet at 200 miles per hour. During the landing, he kept his head above the runway, only 12 inches away. Dempsey's fingers had to be pried from the ladder.

That's called "hanging in there." We all face turbulence in life and come to the point where we don't want to hang in there. The boss makes unreasonable demands, so we start reading the Help Wanted ads.

Someone in church offended us by a chance comment, and we're ready to start looking—again. Our mate treats us like last week's leftovers, and we wonder how a divorce would affect the kids. Some jerk darts in front of us on the freeway, we slam on our brakes, and we're ready to quit being Mr. Nice Guy.

We've reached the end of the rope, and we want to use it to strangle the next "friend" who tells us to tie a knot in it and hang on.

This is where manly Christian character comes into play. The trait of patience gives us the desire and the ability to hang in there. This phrase may not seem like the deep theology it is. As a pastor dealing with people in the worst of times, I find sometimes nothing helps more than the simple encouragement to "hang in there."

Maybe I use it too often. Discussing their difficulties, one church member reassured another, "Hang in there." He received the reply, "You sound just like Tim." I took it as a compliment, but that may be wishful thinking!

As a fruit of the Spirit, patience enables us to avoid being overwhelmed by despair, to control our anger when offended. We don't typically respond that way.

OUR NATURAL TENDENCY: ANGER OR DISCOURAGEMENT

When dealing with problem situations, our old character before Christ frequently responds with either anger or the desire to give up.

Anger

According to Prov. 14:29, patience is the opposite of anger: "A patient man has great understanding, but a quick-tempered man displays folly."

When we're offended, our anger can rise up out of control. We want to give them what they deserve, and maybe just a little more to encourage them never to do it again. But that displays foolishness. We usually make the situation much worse than it originally was, and we burn the bridges of reconciliation. That positive response of anger is the opposite of the tendency to withdraw through discouragement.

Discouragement

When injustice rules, when our money is meager, when failures mount up, we often feel like giving up. The high suicide rate expresses this, as does Ps. 37:7—"Be still before the LORD and wait patiently for him; do not fret when men succeed in their ways, when they carry out their wicked schemes."

The opposite of patience is fretting. We lose heart and get depressed. We get emotionally overwrought. We become tired of always having to strive and fight, only to receive so little.

In either case—anger or discouragement—we wish the problems of life would disappear. But we can't change the outside world we live in—just our inner character.

THE MANLY CHARACTER TRAIT OF PATIENCE

God gives us the ability to respond to life's problems with patience, a part of His character that He imbeds within us. Patience allows us to face trials without anger or discouragement.

Patience Defined

This may not sound like good news, but the literal meaning of patience is "longsuffering"—to continue to suffer from the unfairness of life and not quit, or to "hang in there." Patience has two basic expressions—first, that we use self-restraint in the face of provocation, that we don't retaliate instantly. This focuses on our anger, on patience as the opposite of being quick-tempered. We may have a valid reason to retaliate, but we don't.

Second, patience means we don't surrender to circumstances. We don't quit when life gets difficult. We don't give in to despair. This is the opposite of despondency, when we think there's no way out.

For most of us, these don't come naturally or easily. The only way to consistently express patience is to realize that the source of patience is God, not us.

EXAMPLES OF GOD'S PATIENCE

When we allow the God who lives in us to implant His character in us, then His patience becomes a part of us. Patience defines who God is, according to 1 Tim. 1:16— "I was shown mercy so that in me, the worst of sinners, Christ Jesus might display *his unlimited patience* as an example for those who would believe on him and receive eternal life" (emphasis added).

God restrains himself when we ought to be Post Toasties. He doesn't give up on us, no matter how we disappoint and fail Him. Why? That's His character. And that's the pattern for us. God offers that same patience to be part of your character, but it takes work on your part.

CULTIVATING THE MANLY TRAIT OF PATIENCE

To incorporate patience into your character, you first must consciously eliminate qualities that work against it.

Weed Out

We usually have some very good reasons to blast people or to get discouraged and quit. When we dwell on those valid reasons, patience won't develop. In the garden of our lives, to get the fruit of patience we need to weed out two qualities. The first deals with anger, our desire to get back at people.

Personal Revenge

Romans 12:9-21 tells how to nurture healthy relationships. At the end, verses 19-21, we find a key element: the injunction not to take revenge.

Do not take revenge, my friends, but leave room for God's wrath, for it is written: "It is mine to avenge; I will repay," says the Lord. On the contrary: "If your enemy is hungry, feed him; if he is thirsty, give him something to drink. In doing this, you will heap burning coals on his head." Do not be overcome by evil, but overcome evil with good.

God knows the hearts of people, their motives, their life situations. How many times have we been quick to respond with anger, only later to learn why a person's behavior was understandable?

Back when she was a working single mother, Sundays were especially important to my wife, Sheila. Contact with God refreshed her spirit; contact with others brought support and encouragement. But the hassles of getting a slow-moving teenaged daughter ready on time took a toll on her patience.

Once, already running late, she got stuck on the freeway behind an older couple going well below the speed limit. Frustration at being late to church began building. "Why do people so old even get on the freeway? Why can't they speed up a bit? They're making me late to church!"

Finally an opening in the next lane allowed her to slip in and pass the older couple. She looked over as she passed, ready to wither them with an angry glare, only to discover that it was her beloved pastor and his wife.

Only God can balance justice and grace and not get carried away with emotions. Child abuse most often takes place when an adult overreacts in the white heat of anger, and discipline crosses over the line to abuse.

When God's character changes ours, we must yield the desire for our personal revenge. We leave that up to God. And patience will flourish only when we weed out uncertainty about God's truly being in charge.

Doubts About God

Sometimes our frustration and discouragement grow from wondering if God really is in control of life. *If God truly loved me, would He give me this job just to take it away? If God's in charge of everything, why did I lose my house? Or my car or spouse, or why did my son die at 13, before he had begun to live?*

Discouragement comes when we doubt that God is in control. We see no light at the end of the tunnel. We're not convinced God will work all things out for good. Those doubts destroy patience. Frustration often occurs when we're not convinced God will do the right thing—or even anything. Ps. 40:1 has the solution. "I *waited patiently* for the LORD; he turned to me and heard my cry" (emphasis added).

What was required for God to hear and respond? Patient waiting. Suffering in the circumstances until the time is right for God to step in. When we weed out doubts that God will act, in His best time, then we provide the environment for patience to grow. After our weeding is done, we need to consciously develop the Christian character trait of patience.

NURTURE THE FRUIT OF PATIENCE

We find three key steps in incorporating the patience of

God into our character: focusing on God's presence in our lives, relying on His sovereignty, and developing an attitude of perseverance. The first is found in a verse we already read, Ps. 37:7, that we practice the presence of God.

Focus on God's Presence

David wrote, "Be still before the LORD and wait patiently for him; do not fret when men succeed in their ways, when they carry out their wicked schemes" (Ps. 37:7).

The last part of the verse gives our goal: not to fret over the injustice of life. The first part provides the method: to be still before the Lord and to wait—or to remind ourselves that God is always with us.

When our thoughts continually focus on the real presence of God, then the worries and angers don't seem so oppressive. This is the secret of the victorious Christian life, remembering that the all-conquering King lives within us and works in all things for our good.

Alton Cooper was a big, tough, career Marine. Not one of those little Marines who always has to prove how tough he or she is, Alton just was tough, and everyone sensed it. But as so often is true, inside that gruff exterior lived a soft-hearted man who deeply loved God.

While I was his pastor, exposure to Agent Orange in Vietnam caught up with him. Doctors first thought the cancer in his testicles could be treated, with a good prognosis for recovery. But the cancer spread to his prostate, then his bones. And with the cancer came the pain.

Pain ravaged that once-strong body, but it never touched his spirit. Everyone in the hospital knew Alton loved his Lord. Daily he "made his rounds," visiting other patients with a word of encouragement or expressing thanks to the hospital workers. My own frequent 130-mile round trips brought ministry to me. Despite the pain, Alton had a peace through the suffering.

Finally one of the doctors asked the question: "Mr. Cooper, we know the pain you're in. We know the suffering you're going through. But we just don't know how you have this serenity. What's your secret?"

That was all the opening Alton needed. He shared how his trust in God didn't depend on life going his way, that God had always been there for him. Then he gave the doctor a copy of the following poem:

I met God in the morning,
When my day was at its best,
And his presence came like sunrise
Like a glory in my breast.

All day long his presence lingered,
All day long he stayed with me,
And we sailed with perfect calmness
O'er a very troubled sea.

Other ships were blown and battered,
Other ships were sore distressed,
But the winds that seemed to drive them
Brought to us a peace and rest.

Then I thought of other mornings
With a keen remorse of mind,
When I too had loosed the moorings
With the presence left behind.

So I think I know the secret
Learned from many a troubled day:
You must seek God in the morning
If you want him through the day.

—Ralph Cushman

As your eyes slowly open in the morning, as the fog of sleep slowly drifts away, think of God—as soon as possible. As you head for work, rather than planning your day, spend some time alone with Him. As you come to those daily crossroads, the times of decision, choose what He would have you do. Try to spend each moment of the day in conscious contact with Him.

As you do, being angry becomes more difficult; giving up becomes less desirable. What circumstance of life is as bad as God is good? Cultivating the presence of God enables us to be longsuffering. Second, we also need to develop our awareness of how powerful God is.

Focus on God's Sovereignty

Anger and frustration often grow from a belief that life flies out of control. Patience develops when we understand deep down that God does control life. Our limited vision won't show us that control. But God works to carry out His plan, and nothing can stop that.

Not all that happens matches what God desires. When people die without having given their lives to Him, that violates God's will. According to 2 Pet. 3:9, "The Lord is not slow in keeping his promise, as some understand slowness. He is patient with you, *not wanting any to perish*, but everyone to come to repentance" (emphasis added).

We have free will, and God is sovereign. Job learned that. If you don't know the story, read the book to see how Job faced difficulties that would destroy most of us. At times he thought God had abandoned him. But Job hung in there and learned a vital lesson, which he expressed to God in Job 42:2—"I know that you can do all things; no plan of yours can be thwarted."

God's plan is to work for good in the lives of each believer. According to Rom. 8:28, "We *know* that in all things *God works for the good* of those who love him, who have been called according to his purpose" (emphasis added).

When we have that deep-seated conviction that God will bring good out of the worst situation, we can have patience. We can avoid vengeance, knowing God will do something better than we. We can avoid quitting, knowing that God still works for good. We can avoid despair and discouragement, knowing that someday, somehow, good will come.

Trusting in God's sovereignty allows us to look beyond the tyranny of the now, where difficulties buffet us, and see the long term, where the plan of God is accomplished. Then we develop the character trait of longsuffering. Third, to incorporate the patience of God, we need to have a perseverant attitude.

Develop a "Hang-in-there" Attitude

In Heb. 12:1-3 God gives us the option to "hang in there" regardless of the difficulty:

Since we are surrounded by such a great cloud of witnesses, let us throw off everything that hinders and the sin that so easily entangles, and let us run *with perseverance* the race marked out for us. Let us fix our eyes on Jesus, the author and perfecter of our faith, who *for the joy set before him* endured the cross, scorning its shame, and sat down at the right hand of the throne of God. Consider him who *endured* such opposition from sinful men, *so that you will not grow weary and lose heart*" (emphasis added).

Your race isn't a quick-and-easy 100-yard dash but a grueling, painful marathon. Understand that the good times of life occur far less often than the depths. To see the awe-inspiring view, one must climb the mountain. Life isn't always a stroll in the park. And when one strolls, muggers are often there! But don't quit.

Two frogs on a Wisconsin dairy farm fell into a bucket of cream and couldn't escape. One croaked, "Might as well give up. This stuff is too thick to swim in and too thin to jump out of. We're bound to die, so it might as well be now."

He sank to the bottom and died. But his friend just kept paddling, keeping afloat. By morning he was perched on the mound of butter he had churned. A smile covered his wide face as he ate the flies drawn to the butter.

He hung in there. He didn't quit. And pardon the pun, but he came out on top. If a dumb frog knows enough not to quit, shouldn't you, with the Holy Spirit within, refuse to give in to despair and anger?

COMMIT TO GROW IN PATIENCE

Power alone won't overcome the difficult situations we face. Our tendency in trials is to respond either in anger or in discouragement. And being a Christian doesn't decrease difficulties. Usually they increase.

But we Christian men hang in there. We don't stay discouraged. We don't take revenge. We're in for the long haul. Why? Because God lives within us and gives us His own character trait of patience. Work through the following questions as an aid to building patience into your character.

BECOMING MORE MANLY

1. Describe several times recently when you just wanted to crawl into a hole and hide. What helped keep you out of the hole?

2. What most easily gets you angry? Is that anger caused by the situation, or is it your choice? Defend your answer.

3. What is your working definition of patience? Is it closer to the Bible's definition or to the world's?

4. On a scale of 1 to 5, with 1 representing "I have no patience" and 5 representing "I most often respond with patience," what would be your score? What would you like it to be?

5. What weeds most threaten to choke out patience in your life? What can you do to pull these weeds?

6. Think back on a recent experience when you wanted to get back at someone who wronged you but you didn't do it. How can you use that as a pattern for developing patience into a trait?

7. Describe several times when God showed His patience to you. How did that make you feel?

8. What are your beliefs on the sovereignty of God? Support your answer with Scripture.

9. How can those beliefs help you hang in there in difficult times?

10. With your small group, spouse, or a close friend, talk over one decision you have made to allow patience to grow in your life. How can they help you in this? Be specific.

5
KIND TO
THE BONE
THE MANLY TRAIT OF KINDNESS

The fruit of the Spirit is . . . kindness.
Galatians 5:22

HER BEAUTY ENABLED HER to manipulate men, and she did so with artistry. His leadership skills placed him in the position of guiding the nation, but he matched that with a weakness for the ladies. They made a perfect match. Her attractiveness became so well known that, centuries later, commercials featured her. His legendary strength made his name the standard for strong men.

She discovered combining kindness with her beauty turned men into putty, and she gave just enough of herself to dig her hooks in deep. Their names? Samson and Delilah. Their story is told in the 16th chapter of Judges.

But Delilah's kindness had a dark side. Unknown to Samson, she sold him out to his enemies. If she could discover the secret of his great strength, 5,500 shekels of silver would change hands. She was the original big-money athlete. In the next chapter, a priest hired himself out for just 10 shekels—for an entire year. (But then, he also got room and board! And athletes have usually been paid better than the professionally religious.)

She wined and dined and loved him, finally finagling the secret out of him. He couldn't forever resist her beauty and kindness. She ended up with the money. He ended up with death. Delilah's kindness led to Samson's demise.

OUR NATURAL TENDENCY: ARTIFICIAL KINDNESS

Before we get too righteously indignant at Delilah, don't some of us men share her trait? Do we also manipulate with kindness? Are we nice to people who can benefit us? Do we discount or ignore those who can't? When people treat us nicely, do we respond with niceness? And when others are rude and unforgiving, are we rude and unforgiving in return?

We've all known men who are "bad to the bone." They seem to live by the motto "If you can't say something good about a person, talk all you want." Their guiding principle is "Do unto others before they do unto you." A mean streak defines their characters; they delight in bringing grief to others.

Even as Christian men, we may recognize similar patterns in ourselves. Whether we acknowledge a mean streak within us or merely recognize that we use surface kindness to manipulate people, we miss being what God designed us to be. God wants His men to be different.

Rather than meanness, God desires that we have kindness so deep within our character that we truly are "kind to the bone." We're designed by God to have kindness flow from our inner character to our outward behavior.

We may not be "mean to the bone," but we each need to be transformed by God living within so that kindness abounds. Kindness truly isn't natural for all men. At least deep-seated kindness doesn't define us. We're a curious mixture of kindness and meanness. Sometimes we act with great altruism and sacrifice; the next moment we become petty and selfish. Both extremes represent true parts of who we are. But God desires something better for us: the consistent, manly character trait of kindness.

THE MANLY CHARACTER TRAIT OF KINDNESS

When God's Holy Spirit lives within us, He imbues us with God's character. One of God's traits is that of kindness. We have the opportunity to become "kind to the bone," to have kindness not just as a small part of our identity but as a key distinguishing feature.

KINDNESS DEFINED

The biblical word in Gal. 5:22 translates into the English words "gentleness," "goodness," and "excellence." Kindness means we work well with people without being harsh, hard, sharp, or bitter. The word is often found next to love. Probably we best understand the character trait of kindness as we examine the scriptural examples of God and kindness.

EXAMPLES OF GOD'S KINDNESS

I find very few verses that describe God's character as simply kind. Rather, God and kindness are usually linked together behaviorally. Verses tend to read, "God *showed* his kindness by . . ." God's inner kindness expresses itself in what He does. Several intriguing aspects come out in how God demonstrates kindness. First, God's kindness reaches out to all, not just to some people.

Kind to All

When we act as God does, we show we truly are His children. According to Luke 6:35, God acts in kindness without regard to our worthiness.

Love your enemies, do good to them, and lend to them without expecting to get anything back. Then your reward will be great, and you *will be* sons of the Most High, because *he is kind to the ungrateful and wicked* (emphasis added).

We become children of God when we act like our Father, in kindness toward ungrateful enemies. Here we find the difference between doing *some kind things* and being *a kind person*. Everyone, even Delilah, does some kind acts. Anyone can be kind—when it benefits him or her—toward the people he or she gets along with.

But kindness flows from our character when we consistently act in kindness toward those who don't deserve it. Does God show kindness only to people who deserve it? Of course not. That yields an important principle.

We don't receive God's kindness on the basis of our merit but on the basis of His character. God is kind. Therefore, He acts in kindness. The kindness isn't conditional upon the recipient but the character of the giver. An example of God's kindness is how He gives the blessings of nature to all people.

Blessings of Nature

In kindness, God offers all people the benefits of the natural world. Again, this is not based on merit. Paul the Apostle expressed that to a group of unbelievers in the city of Lystra: "He has *shown kindness* by giving you rain from heaven and crops in their seasons; he provides you with plenty of food and fills your hearts with joy" (Acts 14:17, emphasis added).

God doesn't yield the blessings of nature just to godly people. Why? Because He's kind, and by nature He shows kindness to all. That's God's motive for the second aspect of His kindness—that He offers salvation to all people.

Life in Christ

Titus 3:4-6 combines God's kindness, as an expression of his character, and our own unworthiness to have earned salvation:

When the *kindness and love of God* our Savior appeared, he saved us, not because of righteous things we had done, *but because of his mercy*. He saved us through the washing of rebirth and renewal by the Holy Spirit, whom he poured out *generously* through Jesus Christ our Savior (emphasis added).

God sent His Son to die such a terrible death, because in His kindness He saw the greater good. God's kindness causes Him to consistently act in the best interests of humanity. The Titus passage stresses that we don't receive kindness due to our greatness but because of God's character.

But—God's kindness has a condition upon it. To receive the full measure of the kindness available to us, we need to persevere in our relationship with Him.

Contingent on Continuing

Romans 11:22 reveals two almost contrasting character traits of God, neither of which we dare ignore.

Consider therefore *the kindness and sternness of God*: sternness to those who fell, but kindness to you, *provided that you continue* in his kindness. Otherwise, you also will be cut off (emphasis added).

God offers kindness to all, freely. He can't help but act in accord with His character. But for us to receive His kindness requires having an abiding relationship with Him. No abiding, no receiving. That's the clear sense of that passage. God acts in kindness, but it takes a response from us to take advantage of His kindness.

Think back on God's kindness. Flowing from His character, it extends to all people as a fruit of who He is. Since He's naturally kind, He almost can't help it. Now let's change our perspective from how God shows His kindness to how we show our kindness.

OUR KINDNESS

Kindness doesn't denote the character of most of us men. Nor can we give either the blessings of nature or eternal life to others. But we can develop the character trait of kindness, and we can demonstrate that. Our kindness expresses itself somewhat like God's kindness. Our goal is to examine biblical demonstrations of human kindness. Kindness demonstrates itself in concrete acts toward people.

Helping People

When kindness abides in our character, we'll aid people in distress and pain. Acts 3 tells of a beggar at the gate of the Temple. Crippled from birth and relying on begging for money to support himself, he plied his trade when Peter and John strolled by. Remember—these two were in ministry. Television ministries hadn't yet caught on, and the dollars didn't flow in.

But they gave what they could. With a simple statement of "In the name of Jesus Christ of Nazareth, walk," they eliminated the man's career. He didn't seem to grieve over the loss but ran and leaped for joy on his newly functioning legs.

Unfortunately, some of the religious leaders didn't share that joy, calling Peter and John on the carpet to explain, which they gladly did—"If we are being called to account today for *an act of kindness* shown to a cripple, and are asked how he was healed . . ." (emphasis added).

Peter declared that the healing was an act of kindness. With the Holy Spirit residing within them, they possessed both the kindness and power to share for the beggar's benefit what they had. When the Holy Spirit resides in us, when we allow Him to produce His fruit in us, kindness will then change how we treat others. We may not always begin with kindness, we may not always act in kindness, but we'll see more kindness all the time.

The New York Yankees had just endured a tough loss. The bus ride back to the hotel was quiet and gloomy. Trying to lighten things up, utility infielder Phil Linz picked up his harmonica and played a cheerful tune. Manager Yogi Berra stormed back, berated Linz, and fined him $250. Quite a sum in the days before mega-salaries!

In the off season, Linz received his contract offer in the mail. Along with a decent raise was a bonus check for $250—with instructions from Berra to spend it on harmonica lessons.

Berra acted in kindness. Kindness doesn't mean we never get upset or angry but that we make up for it when we do. Kindness is doing the things necessary to get along smoothly with people. Kindness also affects our speech.

Pleasant Language

Our language may be the most difficult area for God to transform. Our learned responses become so automatic that we often find it difficult to think before we speak. The quick curse, the angry retort, the frustrated shout seem to flow off our lips. But when kindness permeates our character, our language can express it, according to Paul: "We work hard with our own hands. When we are cursed, we bless; when we are persecuted, we endure it; when we are slandered, we *answer kindly*" (1 Cor. 4:12-13, emphasis added).

When people curse us, our kindness allows us to give them better than they gave us. (Better in moral quality, not in quantity of cursing!) When people give us a hard time, kindness helps us hang in there. When others say bad things about us, we respond with kind language.

We don't retaliate and strike back. Instead, we strive to increase the amount of kindness in the world by our language, not decrease it. Likewise, our overall relationships experience a change.

Tenderhearted and Forgiving

Kindness allows us to bear with others when they wound us. Kindness and grudge-keeping are incompatible, as found in Eph. 4:32—"Be *kind and compassionate* to one another, forgiving each other, just as in Christ God forgave you" (emphasis added).

Did you notice the source of kindness and forgiving? We gain those from experiencing God's forgiveness ourselves. We share with others what we receive from God. Because God was kind to us, we desire to be kind to others. In kindness we don't hold the past against people.

A normal teenaged guy named Karl struggled often with his dad. Finally attempting to change, he tried to convince his dad that he had changed. The process was slow, and Karl complained to a friend that his dad kept getting historical.

"Hold on," said the friend. "Don't you mean he gets hysterical?"

"No, he's *historical*. He keeps bringing up the past!"

With God's tenderhearted kindness living within us, we don't get historical. We kindly allow people to grow beyond their past. We've seen how kindness is shown both in God and in us, but how do we develop it ourselves?

CULTIVATING THE MANLY TRAIT OF KINDNESS

To fully establish kindness as a character trait, we need to follow two steps. First, we weed out artificial kindness, and then we nurture kindness by allowing the presence of God to transform our character.

WEED OUT SELF-SERVING KINDNESS

Delilah showed great kindness to Samson, but that kindness was to benefit herself. In Gen. 25, Jacob kindly gave some stew to his brother Esau. But that kindness was in exchange for Esau's birthright. In both examples, the giver gave for personal benefit. Like Delilah and Jacob, many of us have learned that the best way to get our way is to be nice and kind. In doing things for others, we don't appear to be selfish.

But we keep track of our kindnesses. And when needed, we call in our chips. "Hey, Fred—remember when I loaned you $100 to get your car fixed? I've got a little problem. Can you call your friend down at City Hall to get my building permit through?"

Is it wrong to ask friends for help? Surely not. That's part of why we're a church body, to support and help one another. But when we are kind just to benefit ourselves, that's not kindness but manipulation. When we use our acts of kindness as subtle blackmail for our benefit, we don't act in true kindness.

Flattery and compliments may look similar on the surface but are polar opposites. Compliments benefit the receiver. Flattery benefits the giver. A gracious, well-chosen compliment can be the essence of kindness, a vital part of the ministry of encouragement. But flattery is selfishness hidden by kindness.

To establish kindness in your character, carefully examine your motives to discover the false fruit of self-serving kindness. Since that comes so naturally, we need to be somewhat ruthless in this weeding process. Are our acts of kindness a pure expression of doing what is right, or are they manipulative?

If our motives are selfish, we need to re-think the process— not to stop acting kindly but to act without regard to reward, out of a kind character. Once we've taken the first step of weeding out selfish kindness, we move on to the second step of enhancing the growth of kindness in character.

NURTURE THE FRUIT OF KINDNESS

Once again, these character traits don't usually appear full grown in our lives. Our role in the partnership with God is to enhance the conditions in the garden of our spirits that enhance the development of each trait. As we need to do with each trait, the first step in nurturing a trait is to cultivate our closeness to God.

Focus on God's Presence

God is kind. That kindness comes out in all His actions. As Christian men, we reflect the kind character of God. The more we cultivate the presence of God in our lives, through Bible study, prayer, and continual contact with Him, the more kindness we'll see in our character. We also need to specifically nurture two aspects of God's kindness, the value He places on people, joined with a commitment to act in kindness to build others.

Focus on the Value of People

We grow in kindness as we think in terms of God expressing kindness to us. God doesn't act in kindness because our great moral fiber demands it. We're not so perfect that God can't restrain himself from acting in kindness! Rather, God sees an innate value within each person, which makes giving kindness the right thing to do.

We don't earn or deserve kindness. But our value as people created by God makes us worthy recipients. We need to develop the same attitude God has. Just as He gives kindness to us, so do we give it to others.

Philippians 4:8 tells us to allow only thoughts that are positive and edifying. It's too easy to have thoughts like *That jerk deserves to be taught a lesson. Cut me off like that in traffic? I'll show him. He sure doesn't deserve to be treated with kindness.*

The kind response would be *He sure doesn't deserve kindness. He's a real jerk. But then, I don't deserve kindness either. And like God, I'm a kind person. I'll treat him with the kindness God uses toward me.*

Radical? Completely. And we men can respond like that only when we experience a character change. That character change comes from consistently looking at people as worthy of kindness. They're not worthy based on their behavior but on the value God places on them. We need to train ourselves to consistently look on people this way. That attitude will change us.

In the 1994 movie *The War*, Kevin Costner plays a Vietnam War vet scarred and traumatized by the brutality of war and killing. His goal in life is to make the world better than he found it, but he grieves because he killed more people than he saved in the war.

The war continues on his return home. His two children experience friction with the six bullying children of another family. While Costner buys cotton candy for his wife and daughter at a fair, his son, played by Elijah Woods, gets beaten up by them once more. Later, as Costner escorts his bleeding son to their car, he sees two of the youngest children from the other family.

He walks over to them, hands them the cotton candy, which they hesitatingly accept. They're not sure just what he's doing, but the lure of candy is irresistible. His ten-year-old son is enraged.

"Do you know who they are? They're the kids who beat me up!"

"I know that," his dad calmly replies.

"Then why'd you give them the candy?"

"Because they look like they haven't been given anything in a long time."

After a series of long and difficult struggles, the son develops the kindness of his father, culminating in a courageous act that transcends all the previous friction. What's the point? It's that kindness should be given to all, that kindness has the inherent power to transform life.

That's the pattern for us. As you confront a situation, before you act, you can remind yourself both of the importance of others and of your need to act with kindness. That repeated valuing of others will build itself into your character. The next logical step is treating people as God does.

FOCUS ON BUILDING PEOPLE UP

We won't be allowed into another's growth process until he or she perceives that we value him or her deeply as a person. Kindness is the key, according to Eph. 4:29, 32.

> Do not let any unwholesome talk come out of your mouths, but only what is helpful for building others up according to their needs, that it may benefit those who listen . . . *Be kind and compassionate* to one another, forgiving

each other, just as in Christ God forgave you (emphasis added).

Just as God gave himself to aid our spiritual growth, so we need to do it to others. We're commanded to involve ourselves in the growth process of others. One way we build others is from our kind language to and about them. And as we act in kind ways to build others up, something mystical happens.

We grow in kindness toward them. The emotional part of kindness follows our mental attitude and physical actions. When we pray for people, when we act to help them grow spiritually, we see kindness grow even deeper into our own character. This is the "training ourselves in godliness" that we mentioned earlier.

COMMIT TO GROW IN KINDNESS

By our kind language, by our refusal to retaliate, by our tenderhearted forgiveness to one another, by valuing people as God does, we build kindness into a trait that extends deep down into our character. By repeatedly valuing others and by working to build them up, we see kindness in our inner person. Just like our Father.

I encourage you to work through the following questions as part of the process of building kindness deep into your character.

BECOMING MORE MANLY

1. Think back on a time when you were kind to another, but for your benefit. What were your feelings afterward—pride at how well you did it, or guilt? Why did you feel that way?

2. Describe several times when God showed kindness to you. How did that make you feel?

3. What is your working definition of kindness? Is it closer to the Bible's definition or to the world's?

4. On a scale of 1 to 5, with 1 representing "I have no kindness" and 5 representing "I most often respond with kindness," what would be your score? What would you like it to be?

5. Does it bother you that God is kind to all people, even His enemies? Is that fair? Explain your answer.

6. How would someone listening to your conversations rate you on kind language? What can you do to improve in this area?

7. When is it most difficult for you to be tenderhearted and forgiving? Discuss that.

8. What weeds most threaten to choke out kindness in your life? What can you do to pull these weeds?

9. Based on how kind you are to people, how highly do you value others? Are you happy with your answer?

10. With your small group, spouse, or a close friend, talk over one decision you have made to allow kindness to grow in your life. How can they help you in this? Be specific.

6
MORAL FIBER
THE MANLY TRAIT OF GOODNESS

The fruit of the Spirit is . . . goodness.
Galatians 5:22

THE TITLE CHARACTER IN THE COMIC STRIP
Broom Hilda is an ugly yet somehow lovable witch. Her friend Irwin, the troll, has all the innocence and naiveté needed to be truly attractive. One day Broom Hilda asks, "Irwin, what would be the best way to make the world better?"

Irwin thinks for a moment and replies, "Start with yourself! Give up your bad habits and evil pleasures. Then when you're good, when you're perfect, you'll stand as a shining example to others!"

Broom Hilda swiftly responded, "What's the second-best way?"

Can you relate to Broom Hilda? Most of us want to be good. But not too good. And not all the time.

Men seem to have largely abandoned moral fiber. We've lost our moral compass, a reliable source of right and wrong, and we drift. In our age of relativism, each chooses what's good according to his desires.

A Los Angeles Raiders football player got away with a cheap shot in the '94 season. The hit was late, unneeded, and intended to hurt the opponent. The camera caught it, the instant replay showed it, but the officials missed it. No penalty was called. As many commentators castigated him in the following furor, he replied, "It's a dirty hit only if you get caught. I got away with it."

He had his standards of right and wrong, and he felt comfortable with them. Aren't we all like that? Deep within each person lives the concept of good and evil. We may vary in the specifics of what we say is good, but we all have inner standards that determine our morality.

We choose our standards. We may choose to accept the standards we've been taught by parents, the Church, the schools, or our peers. We may choose to create our own personal standards. But we make it clear—we choose. We decide what we accept as good or evil. We tend to reject the concept that there is an absolute definition of good from a source outside ourselves.

A 1991 Barna study revealed only 28 percent of Americans strongly believe in absolute truth. More frightening, only 23 percent of Evangelical Christians accept absolute truth. Perhaps that's part of the reason that the behavior of Christians often is worse than the behavior of unbelievers, as the study in the opening of the book disclosed. If nothing is always true, then our sense of good can change. By that perspective, sometimes sex outside marriage is wrong, and sometimes it's acceptable.

In this environment, good is usually what pleases or benefits us and what we have the ability to get away with. But it's not the same for all individuals. Each person defines his or her own good. Getting a hold on what's good compares to trying to grab smoke with our hands. We smell something but hold nothing.

In contrast, God offers an innate, absolute goodness that flows from His own character. When the Holy Spirit lives within, one of His fruits is goodness—goodness that flows from the character of God.

By definition, we Christian men desire to build God's goodness into the core of our character. That task is made more difficult with the pressures from the world around us to either choose evil or to choose such a relativistic definition of good that the concept of good loses all meaning.

OUR NATURAL TENDENCY: WE GO FOR EVIL

From the perspective of God being the only source of absolute good, we men face four basic options in choosing good and evil with our lives. We can deliberately choose what we know is evil, or we can choose to establish our own standards of good. We can also choose to appear good by God's standards while at the same time refusing to move toward inner goodness. Last, we can choose to be good, as God defines goodness.

Of the four, only one is a true choice for absolute goodness. By default if not intent, each of the other three is a choice for evil. Let's examine each of these options.

CHOOSING KNOWN EVIL

Dwight L. Moody once said, "I have had more trouble with myself than any other man I have met." We could all echo that. But some people major in evil. Evil dominates their character. Paul's statement in Rom. 3:10-13, 23 may have a hint of exaggeration, but basically it's true:

As it is written: "There is no one righteous, not even one; there is no one who understands, no one who seeks God. All have turned away, they have become altogether worthless; there is no one who does good, not even one" . . . for all have sinned and fall short of the glory of God.

Evil persons recognize right and wrong and knowingly choose the wrong. They believe the benefits of evil outweigh the disadvantages, usually assuming that the consequences will never catch up to them. A paraphrase of a wine commercial humorously expresses that "No man goes before his time—unless, of course, the boss leaves early." Good is what you can get away with—remember?

Others believe the advantages of evil exceed the costs, even if they're caught. That would be like robbing a Brinks truck of $5 million, hiding the money, serving 10 years, then getting out a rich man. If I were to try that, legal fees would eat up all the money! Many are willing to face eternal hell for a lifetime of pleasure here.

When continually repeated, evil choices can build a callous around a person's conscience until it's functionally dead. While all people make some evil choices, others choose it so frequently that they become evil. Charles Manson and Adolf Hitler are just a few who appear to have been in this group. I'm sure you suspect some friends or family members who might be included as well!

CHOOSING OUR OWN STANDARDS OF GOOD

Probably the largest of the four groups include those who want to be good, but by their own definition. "I'm a decent person. God couldn't keep me out of heaven. I'm not perfect, but I've never killed anyone. I'm faithful to my wife. The only time I cheat is with the IRS, and that really doesn't count. Maybe I don't go to church, but I worship God in my own way."

And let's be honest—they indeed do some good things. They have some goodness in them. But not enough, because they possess no solution to the evil that still lives within them. They try to "establish their own [righteousness]," as mentioned in Rom. 10:3.

The inadequacy of their situation is described in Eph. 2:8-9—"For it is by grace you have been saved through faith—*and this not of yourselves*, it is the gift of God—*not by works*, so that no one can boast" (emphasis added).

Although they don't intentionally or knowingly choose evil, they don't choose God's good and end up in evil's camp. The next group comes close in numbers to this last one.

CHOOSING THE APPEARANCE OF GOOD

Hypocrites want to appear good, while still doing evil. The word "hypocrite" comes from the Greek word for "actor." Dramas were often performed in large amphitheaters, before the days of binoculars and opera glasses. The crucial facial expressions couldn't easily be seen by much of the audience, so the actor would hold up a mask.

A mask with a smiling face showed comedy or happiness. A mask with a frowning face denoted tragedy or sadness. Today our symbol for drama combines these two masks of comedy and tragedy.

But in time the word "hypocrite" acquired a moral meaning, for those who attempt to appear different on the outside than they are on the inside. Hypocrites want to look good and do evil, as found in Matt. 23:27-28.

> Woe to you, teachers of the law and Pharisees, you hypocrites! You are like whitewashed tombs, which look beautiful on the outside but on the inside are full of dead men's

bones and everything unclean. In the same way, on the outside you appear to people as righteous but on the inside you are full of hypocrisy and wickedness.

I believe these are the "lukewarm believers" of Rev. 3:14-16, whom Jesus will spit out of his mouth. The Lord doesn't want anything to do with people who only want to appear good while holding onto evil. He abhors that intellectual dishonesty. But there's another option.

CHOOSING GOD'S GOODNESS

Some choose deep-down goodness, an absolute goodness defined by God. These people want to do what's right and good. They don't claim perfection, but they have a passion to get closer to it.

Probably the fewest in number of all four groups, this group is our focus: those who commit their lives to goodness and are willing to pay the price. They deeply desire the Christian character trait of goodness.

THE MANLY CHARACTER TRAIT OF GOODNESS

More than our just "doing some good things," God wants us to be good deep down in our character. He desires that we possess a holy passion for purity.

GOODNESS DEFINED

Goodness is a deep-seated desire to be upright, virtuous, praiseworthy, pure, and holy. That's quite a task, but our desire is the key, that we want this to become imbedded in our inner person.

For many, goodness is whatever they decide is good. For the Christian, goodness flows from the character of God. God defines goodness by what He is.

EXAMPLES OF GOD'S GOODNESS

Matt. 19:16-17 offers several insights, including a statement of unity between the Father and the Son. But the main point reveals the goodness of God the Father.

Now a man came up to Jesus and asked, "Teacher, what good thing must I do to get eternal life?" "Why do you ask me about what is good?" Jesus replied. "There is *only One who is good*. If you want to enter life, obey the commandments" (emphasis added).

Jesus proclaims both that goodness fills God's character and that goodness flows from God. God doesn't just do good things—He *is* good.

God wants to get the process of becoming good started. We develop goodness in our character with our desire to be filled with the goodness of God. The Bible records several examples of individuals who became so involved in that process that they were described as good.

EXAMPLES OF GOOD PEOPLE

Some have allowed God to live so deeply in their lives that goodness denotes their character. We'll examine two cases to get a better picture of what it means to be good. First, in Matt. 25 Jesus tells the story of three workers, each given some of their master's property to use and develop for the benefit of the owner.

The first two did well, investing for a return of profit on the principal. The third was afraid to fail, merely hiding the money so it wouldn't be stolen.

When the owner returned to settle accounts, he evaluated the work of the first two: "Well done, *good* and faithful servant!" (Matt. 25:21, emphasis added).

What made them good? An active passion to do what the owner wanted. They established a goal for their lives: to work for the benefit of the owner. They then used what they had to reach the goal. They were faithful in carrying it out.

But the third wasn't praised. In verse 26 we read that he was called wicked and lazy, the opposite of good. Lazy I can understand. But why was he called wicked? There's no record of embezzlement, fraud, or immorality. Again, why was he wicked? Because he did nothing to advance the cause of the owner.

Transferring this principle to our study, we see that one component of goodness is a passion to actively do what God desires.

Merely avoiding the more noticeable expressions of sin isn't enough to be good. Goodness is positive action, not merely refraining from sin.

Barnabas demonstrated that. Acts 11 reveals how some of the Christians who were scattered by the persecution of Stephen went to Antioch and established a new church. The apostles in Jerusalem sent Barnabas there to check out the situation, and he became a source of great encouragement to them. He soon recruited the former archenemy of the Church, Saul of Tarsus, to work with him at Antioch.

Barnabas was described as "full of the Holy Spirit and faith." At the center of all this is the description of him in verse 24 as "a good man." Notice four traits that made him good.

First, he willingly worked for God, going anywhere and doing anything God led him to do. His entire life was committed to encouraging people in the faith. He even stood up to his close missionary partner Paul when he believed Paul wasn't showing enough forgiveness to John Mark.

Second, Barnabas took a stand against his own self-interest. In Acts 4 we read that he sacrificially gave to the church a field he owned to provide for the needy. He was willing to give up what was his for the benefit of others.

Third, he encouraged people spiritually. Originally known as Joseph, the apostles were so impressed with how he encouraged others that they called him Barnabas, literally "Son of Encouragement." The nickname stuck for the rest of his life as he continued to live it out.

The fourth reason the Bible described Barnabas as good is that he allowed God's Holy Spirit to fill his life. He earnestly desired to be the best God designed him to be, and all his actions came from his faith.

If we put all these ideas together, goodness means to allow God to fill your life with His good character and to give your life to God so He may use it as He desires. Being good means to accept God's standards for right and wrong.

We men need to remember that being evil means to work against God, either actively or by passively refusing to work for Him. Don't forget that the third servant wasn't called wicked because of his sinful lifestyle but because of his refusal to use what he had for the advantage of the owner.

Goodness isn't refraining from sin but acting positively for God. To grow in goodness, we need to eliminate any thoughts, attitudes, or behaviors that are impure or that hinder the work of God in our lives. Now, in practice how do we do that?

CULTIVATING THE MANLY TRAIT OF GOODNESS

To nurture a productive garden where the fruit of goodness can flourish, we must eliminate anything that works against the growth of our character trait. Two noxious weeds must be pulled out.

WEED OUT EVIL

Most of us have at least started to move away from evil. We did so either with our interest in or commitment to God. We've expressed a desire for good in reading this book. But we need to make this a complete step by our decision to eliminate any true form of evil. That's the simple encouragement of 1 Thess. 5:22—"Avoid every kind of evil."

We never truly want to weed out evil until we deeply understand how evil evil is. Evil appears good. If it didn't, why would so many people do so much of it? We are told in 2 Cor. 11:14 that "Satan himself masquerades as an angel of light." Sin has pleasure—it brings some benefits to us. Sin has pleasure for a short time, according to Heb. 11:25.

But in the long run, sin destroys. It destroys the best part of us. Finally, it will destroy our very lives if we give it free rein. I don't encourage you to do an in-depth study of evil, but think seriously about the impact it's had on your life. That may be your evil choices, even the evil choices of others, that touched you.

Establish an abhorrence of evil, stemming from recognizing how destructive it is. Rom. 12:9 tells us, "Love must be sincere. *Hate what is evil*; cling to what is good" (emphasis added).

The only way we can cling to what is good is to hate evil. We begin with a decision of our will to move away from evil.

There's a reason God's Spirit is called the *Holy* Spirit. For us to develop the character traits of God through the fruit of the Spirit, we must weed out our desire for evil.

We begin with our decision to seek good in our character, to avoid every form of evil. And we keep that promise to ourselves daily. We take courage from our victories. We confess our losses. And we continue to stand against evil.

Shane struggled with pornography. On the road with his own business, temptations were ample and successful. Temptation then grew with a new job, which required him to monitor the incoming mail, some of which was porn. No longer did he have to visit a store to see it—now it was in his hands. Resisting the desire to open the pages was like holding back an ocean wave with a plastic rake.

But he grew disgusted with himself at losing the spiritual battles. He didn't like the attitudes that viewing porn brought. He began to hate the evil of porn more than he enjoyed the pleasures it produced.

He learned how to short-circuit the process by taking a stand against evil. At the first opportunity, before temptation built its irresistible pressure, he just said "No." (Silently, since others were usually close by!)

With a decision of his will backed by the power of the Holy Spirit, Shane finally began to win the battle. He took a stand against evil and saw goodness grow.

WEED OUT HYPOCRISY

Hypocrisy is wanting to appear good without paying the price of eliminating evil in our lives. Hypocrisy means we intentionally and continually shun any desire to be the same on the inside as on the outside.

Physics professor Malcolm Smedley had given the same lecture hundreds of times. Each time his old chauffeur, Joe, listened in. One night Joe told the prof that he thought he could do the lecture just as well. The prof didn't believe him but was willing to let him try.

They exchanged clothing, and the chauffeur gave a flawless lecture that received a standing ovation. The master of ceremonies said, "We have a little time left. With the permission of our honored guest, perhaps we can spend that in a question-and-answer session."

The chauffeur couldn't even understand what the first question was about but was quick on his feet. He replied, "That question is so simple. I'm surprised such a question would even be asked in such a learned assembly. That question is so basic, I'm going to ask my chauffeur to come up and answer that one."

Our hypocrisy probably won't have such an easy solution! The true solution to hypocrisy is to realize that what we think we hide, the internal evil we don't want to deal with, really isn't hidden at all. Heb. 4:13 tells us, "Nothing in all creation is hidden from God's sight." But what Jesus said in another passage, Luke 12:1-3, causes even more fear to hypocrites:

> Be on your guard against the yeast of the Pharisees, which is hypocrisy. There is nothing concealed that will not be disclosed, or hidden that will not be made known. What you have said in the dark will be heard in the daylight, and what you have whispered in the ear in the inner rooms will be proclaimed from the roofs.

God sees and discloses our internal reality. That totally eliminates hypocrisy, the intentional difference between the outward appearance of good and inner clinging to evil. Those who attempt to hide their evil rather than deal with it will find that inner evil revealed anyway.

If our heart desires to be good, we weed out the evil of hypocrisy with an honest confession of who we are. We have a transparency before God and man. We don't pretend to be better than we are.

We can help one another do this. One of the greatest reasons for hypocrisy is the fear that if others really knew the evil within, they couldn't love and accept us. So as we love others unconditionally, as we accept them with their imperfections, we give them the freedom to share with minimized risk.

Christian men are intended to be wounded healers, working together toward goodness by admitting the struggles within. Ironically, only as we admit our shortcomings, failures, and sin can we experience victory over them. One of our most important steps in growing in goodness is to admit our inner reality. But we can't just eliminate evil—we must replace it with good.

NURTURE THE FRUIT OF GOODNESS

Since goodness doesn't come naturally to us, we must learn what it truly is. And because good flows from God's character, we thereby nurture good in our lives as we study the words of God, as we see His heart, and as we commit ourselves to do His good.

Focus on the Words of God

Our consciences are products of what we program into them. They judge if we meet the standards we accept as proper, so they alone can't be relied on. People each have different definitions of what is good. If a person follows his or her standards of right and wrong, his or her conscience will cause no trouble. In fact, it will congratulate him or her on being a fine, moral person. The person's standards may not match at all what God establishes as good, but the person meets his or her own standards and has a sense of moral correctness.

We need something deeper, more reliable, and consistent: a solid, absolute source of morality. Absolute morality can come only from the nature of God. That nature is revealed in the Bible. We are promised in 2 Tim. 3:16-17 that all we need for complete spiritual lives is found in God's Word. As we learn the words of God, we learn His definition of good. That definition needs to be implanted in our consciences.

The Bible yields two types of passages that reveal what's good: general principles and specific commands. A general principle would be Jesus' statement in Matt. 22 that the two greatest commandments are to love God and love people. He said all the other commands hang on these two.

Specific commands, such as the prohibition of sexual intercourse outside marriage, are examples of the best way to express the general principle of love in those specific situations. We look first for a specific command, then for a general principle that applies.

When we're faced with a moral choice, we first discover what God calls good in the situation, either from principle or command. We don't rely on our untaught natural conscience, nor our emotions, nor our preference, nor what others have taught us. These are all much too vulnerable to serve as primary sources of good, so we search the Scriptures to discover that.

The Bible establishes the foundation for morality, for knowing the difference between right and wrong. The better we know the Bible, the better we know what God calls good. This is the beginning point as we program our consciences with this.

But we need to go beyond merely learning what the Bible says about a situation. In our technological world of today, often no biblical command or principle applies clearly. What's most moral regarding in vitro fertilization? Genetic engineering? These issues are never specifically addressed in the Bible. That's why we need to move beyond the letter of the law to the spirit.

Focus on the Heart of God

When we can't find a command or principle for determining good, we can discover and rely on the heart of God. God's heart has absolute purity toward good and an absolute revulsion toward evil.

That's what we need: a heart that loves good and despises evil, just as God does. This knowledge of the heart of God comes with maturity, based on a thorough knowledge of the Bible and a long-term walk with God.

I believe this is what Heb. 5:14 refers to—"Solid food is for the mature, who by *constant use* have trained themselves to *distinguish good from evil*" (emphasis added). Once we've worked through the "milk" stage, we begin to sense from God's Holy Spirit within us what He desires.

Be careful—this principle *does not* exclude vigorous study of the Bible. This isn't a shortcut to getting our desires met. Rather, it's a mature form of the advice our parents often used on us as children: "Do what Jesus would do."

You know something? There's a lot of wisdom in that. It can be abused, but it can also help us greatly. We begin with "milk," evaluating each situation in light of what the Bible specifically teaches about good. By the "constant use" of running each case through the filter of what the Bible teaches as good, we then train ourselves to recognize the difference between good and evil. Over time, that procedure gives us an inner sense of right and wrong, because God's heart is in us, building into us His character trait of goodness.

Once we have that sense of the good, we need to act on it.

COMMIT TO GROW IN GOODNESS

We commit to grow in the character trait of goodness when we determine to do what's good. Period. Regardless of the cost. You see, our acts reveal what we truly believe. By looking at our outward goodness, people can see the reality of our inner goodness.

God has a work of art in progress—our lives. We cooperate with Him in that endeavor. The final product is a character filled with goodness, with moral fiber—until, at the end of our lives, God looks at us and sees only goodness.

We gain that inner goodness by cooperating with God in chipping away at anything that doesn't match God's standard of goodness. In our inner thoughts, our outward behavior, we move toward goodness.

Look forward to the great day you stand before the throne of Christ and hear Him repeat those glorious words "Well done, *good* and faithful servant. Come and share your Master's happiness."

Working through the following questions will help you in your goal of incorporating moral fiber deep down into your character, and in hearing that praise from Christ.

BECOMING MORE MANLY

1. What is most difficult for you in choosing deep-down goodness?
2. Why is the concept of absolute truth essential to developing goodness?
3. Of the four ways we usually approach evil (choosing known evil, choosing our own standards of good,

choosing the appearance of good, and choosing God's goodness), which did you usually gravitate toward in the past? What is your heart's desire now?

4. What is your working definition of "goodness"? Is it closer to the Bible's definition or to the world's?

5. On a scale of 1 to 5, with 1 representing "I have no goodness" and 5 representing "I most often respond with goodness," what would be your score? What would you like it to be?

6. What aspect of God's goodness most intrigues you? Why?

7. What single aspect of goodness in people most attracts you? Why?

8. What weeds most threaten to choke out goodness in your life? What can you do to pull these weeds?

9. What can you do this week to better understand God's goodness?

10. With your small group, spouse, or a close friend, talk over one decision you have made to allow goodness to grow in your life. How can they help you in this? Be specific.

7
KEEPING COMMITMENTS
THE MANLY TRAIT OF FAITHFULNESS

The fruit of the Spirit is . . . faithfulness.
Galatians 5:22

ALTHOUGH SHE WAS BOTH INTELLIGENT and attractive, Sharon never dreamed of conquering the world, establishing a name for herself, and accumulating great wealth. She merely wanted to marry her high school sweetheart and have children—definitely in that order. She yearned to build a family, to grow old together with her husband.

But Nick decided to break faith. The marriage vows of "until death us do part" went the way of the dinosaur when he realized that many other relationships were available. He felt confined in just one.

With his decision, her dreams of a lifetime came crashing down. Her worst nightmares never put her in the role of a divorced woman, and she struggled with her self-image. Her two boys grew up without their dad—he was always too busy playing to spend time with them. Financially, she was pinched as a single parent, working full time but still having to live in a government-subsidized apartment. Why? A man broke his commitment.

The issue is faithfulness, keeping the commitments we've freely entered into. Half of all marriages fail in their commitment to be together until parted by death. Verbal contracts aren't enforceable; our word is no longer our bond. Even written contracts are broken.

Faithfulness touches the Church. About 60 percent of Americans claim to be Christians. Yet only 40 percent regularly attend church. In California only 20 percent do so. The valley I live in

93

has only 12 percent attendance. The God these Christians claim to follow says our faith needs a connection with a local church. What's happened?

We can get more personal. In most of our churches, only about half of the total members attend worship each week. And of those who attend church, which gender do we most often find? Women. Not men. What's the problem? Unfaithfulness.

God cares about that. One of the character changes He wants to make in us deals with faithfulness—faithfulness that will impact our marriages, faithfulness that will impact our churches, faithfulness that will impact our work. God wants us to be people of integrity, who keep our commitments. Too often that goes against our grain.

OUR NATURAL TENDENCY: UNFAITHFULNESS

Unfaithfulness runs through the Old Testament book of Malachi. The people of Israel returned to Jerusalem from their Babylonian captivity and rebuilt the Temple. But they had neglected to finish the protective walls of the city. In addition, their overall religious practice had declined. What was at the core of this unfaithfulness? It was the leaders, according to Mal. 2:7-9.

"The lips of a priest ought to preserve knowledge, and from his mouth men should seek instruction—because he is the messenger of the LORD Almighty. But you have turned from the way and by your teaching have caused many to stumble; you have violated the covenant with Levi," says the LORD Almighty. "So I have caused you to be despised and humiliated before all the people, because you have not followed my ways but have shown partiality in matters of the law."

The leaders failed to live up to the commitment they accepted to be spiritual guides. As you read through Malachi, you see that they consistently offered poor quality in serving God, just as many leaders today break faith.

After several years as an associate minister, Nolan was being interviewed for the position of senior pastor at another church. A discerning elder asked the young minister how long he planned to stay. With firmness and a winning smile, he said he wanted to end his ministry there. He brought eagerness, enthusiasm, and skill in preaching. He and the church fit together well. The church grew in numbers and in health.

Then a larger church became aware of his preaching ability and called him as its pastor. He truly believed God was leading. Surely the greater salary to take care of his growing family was confirmation. But reality at the new church didn't quite match what he had been told, and he longed for "the good old days." During this time his former church brought in a "seasoned minister," someone who truly would end his ministry there and provide stability.

Unfortunately, he just wanted to quietly finish out his time before retirement, and the church lost its momentum. Why? Several men broke their commitments.

When the leaders break faith in serving God, the people follow. To paraphrase the old nursery rhyme, "And everywhere the shepherds went, the lambs were sure to go." Look at the next verse, Mal. 2:10—

Have we not all one Father? Did not one God create us? Why do *we profane the covenant* of our fathers by *breaking faith* with one another? (emphasis added).

The following verses specifically show how Judah broke faith, by intermarriage with unbelievers (vv. 11-12), by rampant divorce (vv. 13-15), with physical abuse of spouses (v. 16), and by a failure to tithe (3:9-10).

That sounds suspiciously like the Church in 20th-century North America; we're plagued by the same sins. As the Roper survey in the first chapter revealed, the behavior of Christians is often worse than that of unbelievers. A November 1994 article in the Riverside, California, *Press Enterprise* estimated that only 5,000 families nationwide tithe. While I believe that figure is greatly understated, nearly all would agree that tithing is not the norm in church life.

God doesn't take unfaithfulness lightly. Just as He keeps His commitments, He expects us to keep ours. When the leaders broke faith, they experienced the consequences:

"And now this admonition is for you, O priests. If you do not listen, and if you do not set your heart to honor my name," says the LORD Almighty, "I will send a curse upon you, and I will curse your blessings. . . . Because of you I will rebuke your descendants; I will spread on your faces the offal from your festival sacrifices" (*Mal. 2:1-3*).

In the same manner, Mal. 3:2-3 extends similar consequences to the people who break faith:

> But who can endure the day of his coming? Who can stand when he appears? For he will be like a refiner's fire or a launderer's soap. . . . Then the LORD will have men who will bring offerings in righteousness.

God does not appreciate unfaithfulness. Commitments have vital importance to God. We have all been unfaithful—to God, our families, our churches, our employers, indeed, to ourselves. But by his Holy Spirit living in us, God changes our character to one of faithfulness.

THE MANLY CHARACTER TRAIT OF FAITHFULNESS

We all keep some of our commitments. At the same time, we all fail to keep some of our commitments. We tend to keep those that are easy to keep, which benefit us, or until we change our minds. Rather than sporadic faithfulness, God wants to transform us so that faithfulness is who we are deep down.

God yearns that we be men who want to keep commitments, who work at keeping commitments, and who cooperate with him to accomplish that. Since faithfulness generally doesn't flow from our character, we need to understand what it means.

FAITHFULNESS DEFINED

Very simply, faithfulness is keeping our word, following through on commitments, being reliable, not changing every moment, based on the current trend or what's to our advantage. Faithfulness means that we place a high value on keeping our promises, that our word is our bond and people know they can rely on us to do what we say we'll do. We don't waffle back and forth.

Mel was a worker always on the go, always finding some extra job to bring in a little more money. But that desire for more soon took over. During the week he spent his time as a carpenter, and as a side business, he hired out to mow large fields with his tractor. He agreed with his neighbor Jack to mow a field of wild mustard and weeds for $100, but other jobs got in the way. Despite Jack's calls, he kept putting it off.

When Mel finally got ready, he informed Jack the cost would be $200 since the weeds had gotten larger with thicker stems and would require two passes. Mel thought he had him in a bind, since the deadline set by the fire department for mowing was almost up and Jack probably couldn't find anyone else at such a late date.

Mel figured on an easy extra $100. Jack figured Mel had broken the original agreement. Of the two, Jack was right. Mel had broken faith. And Mel claimed to be a Christian. They attended the same church—when Mel wasn't working on a side job, that is.

Faithfulness gives us the integrity to do the right thing regardless of the personal cost. We carry out our commitments, we sacrifice to keep our promises. We do what we say. For us as Christians, that integrity can fully come from God only.

EXAMPLES OF GOD'S FAITHFULNESS

Psalm 89 proclaims the faithfulness of God. Read the entire psalm on your own. Here are the first two verses:

I will sing of the Lord's great love forever; with my mouth I will make your faithfulness known through all generations. I will declare that your love stands firm forever, that you established your faithfulness in heaven itself (*Ps. 89:1-2*).

Faithfulness flows from the nature of God. Even when we're unfaithful, God remains true to His commitments. Our lack of faithfulness will impact our relationship with Him, but He won't allow that to change His character nor how He remains true to the promises He has made. In 2 Tim. 2:11-13 we are given a fascinating insight into the character of God.

Here is a trustworthy saying: If we died with him, we will also live with him; if we endure, we will also reign with him. If we disown him, he will also disown us; if we are faithless, *he will remain faithful,* for he cannot disown himself (emphasis added).

Notice how Paul seems to change horses in midstream. Speaking of our relationship, if we disown God or withdraw from being his child, God will in turn disown us, or break the relationship. But if we fail to live up to our part of the covenant with Him, if we are faithless, that won't prompt God not to live up to the promises He's made to us.

God will be faithful to His promise to forgive us if we confess our sins. God will be faithful to His promise to welcome us back like the prodigal son. Because God is faithful at the core of His being, He can't do anything different without denying who He is.

God won't change the rules during the game. That would be breaking faith. I well remember a science teacher in junior high school. Although I generally enjoyed school and most of my teachers, this particular teacher and I clashed in a major way. At the start of the semester he told us the requirements to receive each grade. Since I needed a B in citizenship to stay in an honor group, I carefully met the minimum requirements.

Then, one week before midterm grades came out, he changed the rules. The new rules gave me a C, and it was too late to move it up to a B. I knew he directed the change at me, and I was enraged at the unfairness of it. I was also out of the honor group. I vowed revenge.

I made arrangements with the counselor to transfer out of his class at the semester break, and I put my interim plan into effect. He had a facial tick—one side of his face would grimace about once each minute. I remember this now with profound embarrassment, but each time he glanced my way I would look him in the eye and make that same facial tick. Readers, please be gracious to me—I was only 13 years old!

He tried not to look at me, so I learned to stretch my arms when his gaze was close by. The movement would unwittingly attract his attention, and I would get him. Again and again. Some of the students caught on and enjoyed the tweaking of authority's nose. I knew I could deny doing anything if I were ever called on it, and I had only a few weeks to go before I was out of his class.

Then I learned my greatest lesson. Even when teachers are

wrong, they still have power. For some strange reason, the counselor changed his mind about allowing me to transfer out—something about learning to get along with difficult people, and not running.

Was I a better-behaved student the next semester? Of course. I wasn't completely stupid. No more facial ticks on my part, no more intentional provoking. But to this day, more than 40 years later, I remember his unfaithfulness. I've forgiven him, and if I met him today I would ask his forgiveness for being so rude and inconsiderate. That truly was inexcusable. But forgiveness doesn't mask how wrong he was to unfaithfully change the rules.

God won't do that. He's faithful to His promises. If He says something, He'll stick with it. I encourage you to read the Old Testament book of Judges, a gracious 21-chapter story of forgiveness. The pattern stayed the same. Israel would forsake God and cling to evil. God would then turn them over to their enemies. They would come to their senses, repent, and ask God to take them back. He did—each time, over and over again.

I can't tell you how much I appreciate that—because I do the same things. So do you. We need the faithfulness of God. Personally, I'm glad that someone with faithfulness embedded in His character is the Lord of creation. Even though I appreciate faithfulness, I'm not filled with it the way He is.

If I were to experience the repeated betrayals that God has endured, I don't think I could respond as He does.

"You people have pushed me too far this time. I know I said I'd forgive you if you repented, but I never thought you'd do it this often! From now on, we're changing the rules in this game. One mistake on your part, and you're history."

I could see me doing that. But God won't. Why? He keeps the commitments He makes. That's who He is. That's His character. And His people can be the same.

FAITHFULNESS FOR GOD'S PEOPLE

Faithfulness applies only to commitments we make, so only those who make commitments to God are held accountable for keeping them. God doesn't require those with no faith to keep faith. But have no doubt—God expects Christians to be faithful. That's made clear in 1 Cor. 4:2—"Now it is required that those who have been given a trust *must prove faithful*" (emphasis added).

We've been entrusted with Jesus Christ. We've been entrusted with the ability to grow spiritually. We've been entrusted with a ministry, a way to serve God unique to each of us. Are we faithful in that trust we've accepted? We must prove faithful to God, our families, our church, our bosses, ourselves.

God requires a passion for faithfulness. That doesn't mean we can't ever fail. But when a faithful person does fail, he or she acknowledges it to God and to individuals against whom faith has been broken. Then he or she picks up the pieces and moves on ahead, rebuilding his or her reputation as a faithful person.

Faithfulness is difficult. Faithfulness requires saying no to ourselves in order to keep our word. It means sometimes doing without in order to pay the bills we committed to pay. If we want to be God's children, we need to develop the character trait of faithfulness.

CULTIVATING THE MANLY TRAIT OF FAITHFULNESS

First of all, realize that we do what we want to do. We analyze the options, calculate the cost/benefit ratio, and choose what's most important to us. That means we can choose faithfulness and integrity if they're valuable enough to us.

The comic strip character Andy Capp is a lovable Cockney rogue, with the stress on rogue. In one episode he strolled up to the neighborhood eatery and apologized to his waiting friend. "Sorry I'm a bit late, Chalkie, but I was spinnin' a coin t' decide whether I should spend the morning playin' billiards or spend it lookin' for a job."

Chalkie smiled. "An' billiards won, eh?"

Andy replied, "Yep, but it took about 15 throws!"

Sometimes we go through amazing verbal rationalizations just to do what we want. But that process can also be used to build faithfulness. The key is to prioritize our lives, to determine that most of all we want to live up to our commitments, to be a person of our word, where our word is our bond. To nurture the character trait of faithfulness, we need to eliminate whatever works against it.

WEED OUT SHORT-TERM THINKING

For many of us, our wisdom extends no further in time than a week. What do I mean? We often substitute short-term solutions to problems that at best have a long-term character solution. But we get so caught up in the short-term problem that we don't even look for the long-term consequences. This is a character issue.

Here's an example. We've made a number of financial commitments, including the mortgage, that have us stretched to the limit. We get laid off from work and live off our credit cards for several months. Soon, even though we're back at work, we have such a debt burden that we would have to win a sweepstakes to pay it off.

We hear of a bankruptcy attorney, he explains our options, and eliminating our debt looks like instant mental health again. But we tend to ignore two issues. First, bankruptcies have negative long-term financial consequences. Second, and much more important, the character issue of faithfulness intrudes.

We made a commitment to pay these bills. We received something of value, and we agreed to pay for it. As Christians, God expects us to live up to our commitments. Please don't think I'm against all bankruptcies. Our laws allow for debt relief, and lenders factor that in when they make loans and calculate interest. Bankruptcy can be a good, moral solution.

But maybe we're too quick to do something like this, without thinking of the character implications. When we fail to do our absolute best to live up to our commitments, we lose a little piece of character.

If we do that too frequently, those little pieces combine until we lose a major part of our faithfulness. These little events either build or destroy faithfulness in our character. We build our reputations for faithfulness through them.

Do you remember Mel, who mowed Jack's field earlier in

the chapter? Jack was in a bind and paid the extra $100. He had little choice. Mel manipulated the situation masterfully. He thought.

But they lived in a rural area, where people rely on one another and where few secrets live long. Many of the neighbors saw through Mel's trick. They had planned on hiring him until they saw his character. Short term, he made an extra $100. Long term, he lost far more. He lost financially, and he lost his reputation for faithfulness.

If you want to build faithfulness into your character, weed out looking only for what will benefit you in the short term. Decide to look at the long-term character impact. Once we weed out that short-term thinking, we can take steps to build faithfulness into our character.

NURTURE THE FRUIT OF FAITHFULNESS

As with all the character traits, we need to take concrete action in cooperating with God in building that trait. Again, as with all the traits, our relationship with God provides the foundation. Once we focus on the presence of God in our lives, specific steps follow in getting goodness deep down.

Focus on God's Presence

Remember our earlier statement that we do what we want? Many people get fired up about faithfulness at a rally or conference but don't continue to live faithfully. In effect, they place a higher long-term value on pleasing themselves. But when we value the presence of God in our lives above all else, faithfulness follows. In 2 Chron. 19:9 this is expressed: "He gave them these orders: 'You *must serve faithfully* and wholeheartedly *in the fear of the* LORD'" (emphasis added).

Faithfulness is linked to the fear of God. How does that work? When we recognize the transcendence of God, a normal response is to feel just a little overwhelmed and intimidated. That's called "the fear of the Lord." As we realize that God surpasses all else in life, being faithful to Him becomes important. We see He's much more awesome than we are, and we desire to please Him.

Do you remember my difficulty in being faithful to that junior high science teacher? To my immature 13-year-old reasoning, he was no better than I and certainly didn't deserve my faithfulness to him. Other teachers impressed me greatly with their care, education, and fairness, and I had no problems being faithful to their assignments.

In starting the process of becoming faithful deep down, the key distinction deals with the quality of the person we're faithful to. We begin with faithfulness where it's easy to be faithful. We then grow to extend faithfulness to those who don't deserve it. This is where I missed it with my teacher.

Faithfulness begins with realizing just who lives within us. Knowing the ultimate value of the Creator of all, who abides inside us, makes it easier to be faithful. As we nurture the presence of God within us, we grow in faithfulness.

Obedience to God is a vital part of all this. The word for faithfulness is the same as the word for faith—the context determines the meaning. The word for faith also means trust. Can you guess what the Bible consistently links with trust and faithfulness? One of our classic hymns has captured the connection between trusting and obeying. Deut. 9:23-24 also provides an example:

> When the LORD sent you out from Kadesh Barnea, he said, "Go up and take possession of the land I have given you." But you rebelled against the command of the LORD your God. You did not *trust him or obey him. You have been rebellious* against the LORD ever since I have known you (emphasis added).

God gave them the land and the command to possess it. But in rebellion, they were unfaithful. They neither trusted nor obeyed God. In effect, they had no active, deep-down faith in God. A. W. Tozer said, "The Bible recognizes no faith that does not lead to obedience, nor does it recognize any obedience that does not spring from faith. The two are opposite sides of the same coin."

The concept of covenant is crucial. People outside of faith can never be unfaithful to God, since they never made a covenant to be faithful. They never agreed to follow God's laws.

But Christians are different. A covenant is a mutual agreement: you do this; I'll do that. To greatly simplify our covenant with God, our part is to make God number one in our lives, to obediently follow Him, to know Him deeply. God's part is to give us an abundant relationship with Him of forgiveness and grace now, and heaven later.

When we don't come through on our part, we break faith. We compromise our integrity. Obedience says, *God, I believe with all my heart that you know what's best for me. So I'll do whatever you tell me, even if it doesn't make sense to me, even if I can't see any benefit now.*

Disobedience is unfaithfulness. So if we want to build faithfulness to God, we must make a commitment to obey Him. Obedience can be a fiery crucible that burns away unfaithfulness, that brings us closer to Him.

But faithfulness must extend to people as well. We can't show our faithfulness to God without it impacting others. So for faithfulness to be deeply implanted in our character, we need to move from faithfulness to God to faithfulness to people. We build faithfulness to others when we perceive the value they have in God's eyes.

Value People Highly

We find it easier to treat people with faithfulness when we see the value they have. When we see little value in them, keeping our commitments to them becomes less important. That was what I learned with my teacher.

But the mistake I made then, the same mistake many make, is to derive their value from what they do, especially what they do *to* us. If they mistreat us, they certainly don't deserve faithfulness. If they treat us nicely, it's easier to keep commitments.

Fortunately, God treats people faithfully, not in response to their behavior but in line with their inherent value as people. When we value people with the value God places on them, keeping our commitments to them becomes easier.

In Matt. 25:40 Jesus taught that whatever we do to others, we do to Him. Why is that? Our attitudes to God's creation (primarily people, but this can include the physical universe as well) reflects our attitudes to the Creator. God was quite clear—we can't love Him if we don't love His people.

If we desire to treat God with faithfulness, we need faithfulness in our relationships. Think carefully. We must treat others as faithfully as we do God, because in this we are being faithful to God. And, if we're unfaithful to people, we're unfaithful to God.

This principle has some frightening applications. When we tell someone we'll pray for him or her, we had better do it. If we commit to doing something, we had better not only do it but do the best we're capable of. And if something more exciting comes up, we turn it down and explain that we have a previous commitment. If we purchase something on credit, we promise to pay for it.

Otherwise, we don't break faith only with people—we break faith also with God. We don't want to sacrifice the integrity of our relationship with God, even if we must sacrifice pleasure or comfort. I encourage you to carefully examine your life to eliminate any threats to faithfulness.

Examine your marriage. Don't play with the fire of unfaithfulness, or you'll eventually be burned. Examine your job, your friendships. Do they consistently reflect the faithfulness of God?

To build faithfulness deep down in our character, we need to value others as worthy of our faithfulness. Faithfulness needs to be built into our lives, through the process we've worked through. Let's commit ourselves to building faithfulness deep down into our character.

COMMIT TO GROW IN FAITHFULNESS

For us to grow in faithfulness, we need to view ourselves as people of integrity, as bound by our promises. When we see the tremendous value God places on us, then we can understand how we ought to be faithful, because that's a virtue that matches our value. God didn't create us to be selfish slime, committed to sin.

God had something better in mind: that we men have integrity. As Jesus said in Matt. 5:33, our simple yes or no should be relied on, that others recognize us as people of integrity, who live up to their word.

Why should we be like that? Because we're children of the King, a faithful King who created us to be faithful. God placed within us enough value that we shouldn't stain that with unfaithfulness. May we never allow our lack of integrity to destroy the goodness God sees within us.

A lovely villa rests on the shores of beautiful Lake Como in the Italian Alps. A tourist complimented the trusted old gardener, who had maintained the grounds for years.

"The owner must come here frequently," he said.

"No," he replied. "He's been here only once in 15 years, and then I didn't see him."

"But how do you get your orders?"

"From the owner's agent, who lives in Milan."

"Then he must come here often."

"No, not often, perhaps once a year or so."

The tourist was amazed. "You have no one to supervise your work, and the grounds are as neat as if you expected the owner to come back tomorrow!"

The old gardener firmly replied, "Today, sir! Not tomorrow, but today."

That was a faithful man, faithful to his trust. May we choose to be just as faithful to our Lord and one another. Work through the following questions, which can help you in your endeavor to build faithfulness.

BECOMING MORE MANLY

1. Describe a recent experience when someone broke faith with you. How did you feel? How did that impact your relationship with him or her?

2. What is most difficult for you in being faithful? What can you do to improve?

3. What is your working definition of goodness? Is it closer to the Bible's definition or to the world's?

4. On a scale of 1 to 5, with 1 representing "I have no faithfulness" and 5 representing "I most often respond with faithfulness," what would be your score? What would you like it to be?

5. Describe times when God has been faithful to you, and the impact that has had on you.

6. What has God entrusted to you that you desire to be faithful in? How do you act on that?

7. What weeds most threaten to choke out faithfulness in your life? What can you do to pull these weeds?

8. How does the presence of God in your life help you to be faithful?

9. Do you give different values to different people? If so, what standards do you use, and how does that valuing affect how faithful you are to them?

10. With your small group, spouse, or a close friend, talk over one decision you have made to allow faithfulness to grow in your life. How can they help you in this? Be specific.

8
CHOOSING OUR RESPONSE
THE MANLY TRAIT OF GENTLENESS

The fruit of the Spirit is . . . gentleness.
Galatians 5:22-23

SEVERAL YEARS AGO I ATTENDED a Rams' football game, back when they still played in southern California. Probably nothing else so well demonstrates my patience. I've been a long-suffering fan since my teens, through unpopular coaches and owners, through overpaid and pampered players, through many losses, including the mother of all losses in the Super Bowl. The strategy of the game intrigues me, the physical challenges motivate me, and the sporadic wins excite me. Their recent success in St. Louis only drives the dagger deeper.

But I never came so close to getting in a fight as at this particular game. Actually, I've never even come close to fighting at a game. While I stood in line for a hot dog and Coke, a young man in his early 20s just in front of me became verbally abusive to the server. He tried to buy more beers than he was allowed and was just overall obnoxious. Apparently, these weren't his first beers of the day. For some reason he then started in on me. (Maybe it was my gentle encouragement to give the server some slack!)

He saw a graying man in his 40s and must have thought, *Here's an easy mark.* His foul language and challenge to fight provoked a surprising response in me. He didn't realize this 44-year-old had been working out and was stronger than he had ever been. When younger, I had taken some training in boxing. I calmly measured the kid and knew I could take him.

I planned the first, second, and third punches. My conscience wouldn't allow me to throw the first punch, but I knew

just the words to push him over the edge. And most surprising-
ly, I wanted to. I really wanted to. Maybe the physical environment of football played a part in that desire, maybe it was a test
of my new strength, or perhaps it was my increased levels of
testosterone from working out. And my earthly nature con-
tributed a lot. I deeply wanted to teach this young punk a lesson in politeness by flattening him.

But deeper down, I wanted to be gentle, not to respond automatically according to my old nature. Fortified by urgent and
quick prayer, I held back. The onlookers later complimented me
on "doing the right thing," but more than their praise, I desired
the praise of God.

I battled myself in that situation. I'm not a gentle person by
nature. Gentleness has been cultivated only with great difficulty. While in elementary school, I formed and led a gang with
my best friend, Rocky, against some school bullies. I fought frequently. Dad once told me that I might have been the first elementary student ever kicked out of that school for fighting!

Our world is harsh, and we rarely find gentleness. The Rams'
football game demonstrated that. My body felt sore just watching the ferocious tackles and blocks. The evening news brings
reports of violence inflicted on people, from distant lands to our
own streets. Violence seems to be part of the fabric of people.

Again, God offers an alternative, the Christian character trait
of gentleness. The Greek word for this fruit of the Spirit is also
translated into the English "meekness" or "humility." God allows us to change our inner person so we can consistently
choose to respond to the difficulties of life with gentleness.
That's not natural for most of us.

OUR NATURAL TENDENCY

Gentleness will change us in four areas in life: conflict, control, fear, and self-image. After we examine the natural tendency in each of these four areas, we'll then define gentleness according to the Bible.

IN CONFLICT

When faced with conflict, we often respond by attempting to

overpower others. Depending on age, attractiveness, physical strength, or intelligence, the tools we use to do that will differ. But the underlying attitude is *No one pushes me around! I don't get mad—I get even.* That was my initial attitude at the football game, and it's imbedded in our world. We don't naturally respond with gentleness, nor do we expect it in others.

While taking an accident report, a Los Angeles police officer asked the driver of a car how he happened to hit the pedestrian in the crosswalk. The driver replied, "I didn't even touch him. I saw him in the crosswalk, came to a stop, motioned for him to cross, and he fainted."

Gentleness in conflict is so rare. We tend to use force even if we have an alternative. Power is quicker, sometimes easier, and it certainly requires less self-control. That's why the character trait of gentleness is needed: gentleness gives us a better option in dealing with conflict.

Can you imagine the publicity if I hadn't finally brought gentleness to the football game? "Christian minister arrested for brawling at Rams' game. Report at eleven." But maybe there would have been an upside: I might have gotten a shot at the heavyweight boxing championship. George Foreman has proven 40-somethings can fight!

IN CONTROL

We also need gentleness to combat our normal desire to be in charge. When we're too driven to shape our lives, we tend to discount others. Their needs and wounds aren't as important as ours. We can run over people, even when our goals are good.

We men typically can be much too forceful to those who oppose what we want to do. For instance, we may want to be a giver, to help others without allowing them to help us. But when others want to help us, we can feel threatened. Our plan is at risk. We may react much too strongly.

Gentleness can be the antidote to treat others with greater concern, to be less threatened by them.

IN FEAR

We often equate gentleness with weakness. The King James

Version translates gentleness as meekness, and we inaccurately think meek equals weak. Some people appear to act with gentleness, while in truth they're afraid.

A patient at a dentist's office tried to lighten her fear by listing her middle name as "Wimp." The receptionist laughingly agreed that many felt that way. A little later she stepped into the waiting room and said, "The doctor will now see the wimp."

Four people got up.

We all face fear. Some respond by freely admitting it. Others deal with it by running away from the source. But some respond to it by overcompensating. They become angry, hostile, or loud. Many use anger as an effective mask for fear. They operate under the assumption that if they seem to be the opposite, no one will suspect their deep-down fear.

Christian gentleness isn't weakness or giving in to fear. Rather, gentleness uses God's strength to deal with our fear in the best manner, neither as a coward nor a bully.

IN SELFISHNESS

The Greek word for gentleness is also translated "humility." When we believe we're greater and more important than others, our relationships suffer. At that same football game, my friend and I discussed athletes we enjoyed and those we didn't respect. I noticed a common trait in the athletes I didn't care for: arrogance.

Gentleness in the form of humility gives us the ability to have a balanced view of ourselves, to avoid the excess of conceit that some struggle with. Too much pride and self-absorption become roadblocks to deep relationships. Few want to spend much time with those whose main concern is self.

We all face these four natural tendencies. We counter them with God's own character trait of gentleness.

THE MANLY CHARACTER TRAIT OF GENTLENESS

Since we have so many different and unbiblical ideas of gentleness, we need to have a clear concept of what God means by it. That way, our gentleness is defined by God, not by the false concepts we all begin with.

GENTLENESS DEFINED

A working definition of the character trait of gentleness is "a God-given strength to control our attitudes and actions so we can deal with people according to their needs, not according to our own weakness."

First of all, gentleness is a character transformed by God, a character that demonstrates a mildness of disposition, a temperate and considerate spirit. Gentleness enables us to choose the best way to respond without automatically being angry, harsh, or violent.

Gentleness is strength under control. Sometimes gentleness is demonstrated with firmness and power, but that's a godly choice, not a natural reaction. As we've seen, gentleness includes humility, a refusal to place our desires above others.

Our society places a low value on this. People want power and strength, assertiveness. But God has a different perspective on the trait.

EXAMPLES OF GOD-VALUING GENTLENESS

Although we often view gentleness as weakness, God doesn't. He considers gentleness to be a strength of great value and will reward us for it. According to Ps. 37:11, "The meek will inherit the land and enjoy great peace."

The meek end up with all the good stuff! Why? In part it is because they don't tend to kill themselves off, but more so because God cherishes meekness. We can't be weak and accomplish inheriting the land. In the King James Version, Ps. 45:4 tells that God will act majestically on behalf of meekness.

In thy majesty ride prosperously because of truth and *meekness* and righteousness; and thy right hand shall teach thee terrible things (emphasis added).

God will ride in majestic victory for the sake of the meek. "The LORD takes delight in his people; he *crowns the humble with salvation*" (Ps. 149:4, emphasis added).

Who gets saved? The humble. The gentle. The meek. Not the

arrogant, the proud, the haughty, the violent, and harsh people. We see that throughout the Bible, and especially with Moses and Jesus.

Seen in Moses

Numbers 12:3 teaches that Moses was more humble, or meek, than anyone else on earth. But he certainly wasn't weak. Raised in Pharaoh's court, Moses both possessed and used authority. Physically, he had enough strength to kill a man when defending a Hebrew slave. Emotionally, his anger flamed enough to do that.

Later in life, he consistently stood up to Pharaoh, arguably the most powerful man then on earth. Even so, his anger sometimes got the best of him. He had the personal power to lead more than a million former slaves through a wilderness to the edge of the Promised Land.

Was Moses a wimpy weakling? Not at all. He had power and strength, but in his later life it was clearly under the control of God. He didn't cave in to opposition, nor did he use his power selfishly against his opponents. Jesus is the same.

Seen in Jesus

Remember who Jesus is: the creator of the universe, the Son of God, fully divine. At any moment He could call down thousands of angels to carry out His wishes. Yet the prophecy about Him in Isa. 42:1-4 yields a picture of a gentle, quiet, humble person. He had power, but that power was under control:

Here is my servant, whom I uphold, my chosen one in whom I delight; I will put my Spirit on him and he will bring justice to the nations. He will not shout or cry out, or raise his voice in the streets. A bruised reed he will not break, and a smoldering wick he will not snuff out. In faithfulness he will bring forth justice; he will not falter or be discouraged till he establishes justice on earth.

Though he created the universe, Jesus didn't have to be the center of attention, the life of the party. He wasn't loud and boisterous, although He did enjoy a good party. He treated the wounded with tenderness; people received comfort just by His presence. He was gentle with those whose spirit was a flickering spark that could easily be extinguished.

Even so, He was committed to justice. This is the hard edge of gentleness: taking a strong stand for righteousness out of a concern for all people. His gentleness didn't cause Him to ignore wrong and let it go on. Gentleness doesn't cave in to evil but firmly uses the minimum power needed to enforce justice for all.

Both Moses and Jesus had power. Both could get angry. Yet they were in control—they acted in gentleness, just as we should.

Seen in Christian Men

God wants that same gentleness in all His people. That gentleness begins in our new hearts and spreads outward until we consistently act gently. Although 1 Pet. 3:3-4 primarily refers to women, I believe both sexes can possess a beauty that comes from a gentle spirit.

Your beauty should not come from outward adornment, such as braided hair and the wearing of gold jewelry and fine clothes. Instead, it should be that of *your inner self, the unfading beauty of a gentle and quiet spirit*, which is of great worth in God's sight (emphasis added).

That inner tranquility radiates into all we do. This is the picture of a Christian, with gentleness as a central part of his or her character. How do we develop that?

CULTIVATING THE MANLY TRAIT OF GENTLENESS

To become gentle, we first need to decide that since God values gentleness, we will as well. According to 1 Tim. 6:11, we'll never be gentle until it's our passion:

Man of God, flee from all this [selfish motivations], and *pursue* righteousness, godliness, faith, love, endurance and *gentleness* (emphasis added).

We cannot achieve gentleness until we flee selfish motivations. Then we must earnestly endeavor to be gentle, to make it a priority. That's the first step in pursuing gentleness. In our cultivation of gentleness, we then must apply it to those four areas we mentioned earlier.

We struggle with becoming gentle in conflict, control, fear, and self-interest. Our standard format at this point is to examine several weeds that work against gentleness, which we need to pull out, then to look at specific steps to nurture the fruit.

Rather than chopping up the flow with weeding out each of the four areas, then going back to nurturing gentleness in each area, we'll deal with each topic one at a time. For instance, in the area of conflict, we'll see what we need to weed out at the same time we examine how to nurture gentleness in that area. I believe this will make it clearer as we seek to cultivate gentleness in our character.

IN CONFLICT: WEED OUT HARSHNESS; NURTURE RESTRAINT

Because we all have the rough surfaces of imperfection, we rub one another the wrong way and produce heat. Science calls that friction; we call it interpersonal relationships. Incorporating gentleness into our character impacts how we handle conflict with others. Each of the following verses gives a slightly different angle on developing gentleness. First Corinthians 4:21 blends confrontation with sensitivity. "What do *you* prefer? Shall I come to you *with a whip*, or in love and *with a gentle spirit*?" (emphasis added).

A gentle person refuses to unnecessarily use harsh means. But when needed, harshness doesn't contradict gentleness. Paul left the decision to the Corinthians as to his gentleness or harshness. He would be as gentle as they would allow. But if gentleness didn't work, harshness would follow.

The key is not to start with harshness. Spanking children is a good example. Spanking has an effective and scriptural role in discipline. But to be most productive, spanking should be a last resort. We begin with reasoning, time outs, restrictions, and other appropriate measures. But if we start harsh, we can't get more intense without going over the line to abuse.

That principle extends to other relationships as well. We build gentleness into our character when, rather than first resorting to force, we become imaginative in discovering other ways to deal with conflict. Prov. 15:1 tells us, "A gentle answer turns away wrath, but a harsh word stirs up anger."

Our gentle spirit will look for ways to express itself in conflict. So before we automatically respond with harshness, let's slow down to allow God's Holy Spirit to teach us to be as gentle as possible.

Gentleness certainly doesn't mean we ignore other's sins. It isn't the ostrich syndrome, when we just don't want to know what's going on. Remember that Jesus dealt with justice in gentleness. According to Gal. 6:1, we can do the same: "Brothers, if someone is caught in a sin, you who are spiritual should restore him gently. But watch yourself, or you also may be tempted."

Being gentle doesn't mean pretending evil doesn't exist. We deal with it, with the gentlest means that will be effective. Our inner character of gentleness will express itself. Many Christians today miss the injunction of 2 Tim. 2:23-25:

> Don't have anything to do with foolish and stupid arguments, because you know they produce quarrels. And the Lord's servant *must not quarrel*; instead, he must be kind to everyone, able to teach, not resentful. Those who oppose him he *must gently instruct*, in the hope that God will grant them repentance leading them to a knowledge of the truth (emphasis added).

A gentle person avoids quarrels. He may disagree, but he does so agreeably, with respect for the other. We face many conflicts, but we never have a reason not to have an attitude of gentleness.

I'm quite concerned about the tone of public discourse of many Christians. We may be right, but our argumentative spirit wins few allies. Some have polarized the abortion debate by using terms like "baby killers," "repent or go to hell." Often such tactics verge on force.

I believe the Bible supports our position on life beginning at conception. But do we consistently express our beliefs with gentleness, as the last passage commanded us? In many cases, I'm afraid we don't.

When we don't allow people the freedom to disagree without our attacking them, we change few minds. But when we gently and firmly express our beliefs and instruct people with respect, then we transform conflict into something constructive. The key to dealing with conflict is to weed out harshness and nurture restraint, building gentleness into our character.

IN CONTROL: WEED OUT CONTROLLING; NURTURE GOD'S GUIDANCE

By nature, we want to be in control of what goes on around us. When others don't go along with our desires, friction builds. A central tactic in building humility is to weed out our need to control life. Gentleness grows when we give up being in charge and leave that to God. We're not threatened by opposition—that becomes God's problem, and we can rest easy. Ps. 25:9 teaches that: "He *guides the humble* in what is right and teaches them his way" (emphasis added).

Whom does God guide? Those who don't claim to know it all. Those who are open to God's guiding their lives rather than insisting on doing it on their own. The gentle are eager for God to lead. But when people fight for their right to direct their lives, they lose gentleness.

When others appear to interfere with what we want for our lives, we find it hard to respond with gentleness. After all, we have to look out for ourselves—no one else will! That tendency is a weed we must pull out if we want to cultivate gentleness, because otherwise we tend to look on people as opponents when they don't advance our desire for our lives.

We nurture gentleness into a deep-seated character trait as we yield our desires to God. As we accept whatever He brings or allows into our lives, gentleness is able to grow within us. We accept as truth that God is both more knowledgeable and wiser than we are, that His plans for us are better than ours.

When we imbed the promise of Jer. 29:11 into our lives, we build gentleness. "I know the plans I have for you," declares the LORD, "plans to prosper you and not to harm you, plans to give you hope and a future."

When we truly believe that, we don't look on people who oppose us as obstacles to our best. We know God is in charge of that, and we find rest. Gentleness grows as we give up to the Lord the desire to control our lives.

IN FEAR: WEED OUT FEAR; NURTURE COURAGE

We typically respond to fear with either fight or flight, a heightened aggressiveness or a cowardly avoidance. Deep down, both are responses of weakness. True gentleness grows when we face difficulty, are aware of our fears, and stand up for the right with the courage God provides. In doing that, we use only enough firmness or harshness to accomplish the God-given job. That's what Paul did in 2 Cor. 10:1-2.

By *the meekness and gentleness of Christ*, I appeal to you—I, Paul, who am "timid" when face to face with you, but "bold" when away! I beg you that when I come I may not have to be as bold as I expect to be toward some people who think we live by the standards of this world (emphasis added).

Paul faced rebellion in Corinth that prompted fear in him, or timidity. He didn't look forward to the encounter with eagerness. But he faced his fears and clearly told them that the fear wouldn't incapacitate him. He would be just as bold as necessary, despite his own tendency toward timidity.

Paul didn't run away, nor did he respond with heightened aggressiveness. Rather, he had the gentle courage from God within to deal with the problem. Be sure to notice the source of Paul's strength: the gentleness of Christ.

For us, gentleness grows into our character as we face our fears rather than run or overreact. We learn we can stand up and use only the boldness needed. With the Christian character trait of gentleness, we master our fears.

IN SELF: WEED OUT SELFISHNESS; NURTURE HUMILITY

We innately look at life from a personal perspective. When others get in our way, we tend to treat them as opponents, with unkindness. That desire to get our way brings multiple difficulties to our relationships.

Remember that gentleness translates into humility. We build that character trait as we harness our inborn desire to advance ourselves, at the expense of others, with compassion for them. Eph. 4:2 expresses that. "Be completely humble and gentle; be patient, bearing with one another in love."

Humility ought not to be something we occasionally do but something we consistently are. We're completely humble when we bear with others; when we consider their needs on a par with our own; when we're sensitive to their pain and wounds; when in our conversations we aren't simply waiting to get our two cents in, but express our genuine concern for others; when we accept their imperfections, just as we accept our own.

As noted earlier, babies begin with total self-absorption, thinking the world revolves around them. Maturity moves us away from that to balance our needs with those of others. Gentleness grows into a character trait as we humbly value others the way we value ourselves. We regularly act on that value until gentleness builds into our character.

COMMIT TO GROW IN GENTLENESS

Gentleness isn't easy. Nor is it valued by the world. But God wants us to be as gentle as He is. His Holy Spirit living within us will transfer that trait into us. He will help us not to respond with harshness in conflict; to give up our desire to control things; not to run or get overly aggressive when we fear; to value others as we value ourselves.

In other words, we must not simply do some gentle things but must be gentle *people*—not wimps, not cowards, not bullies, not selfish, just gentle people who face adversity with godly courage and control.

After a tiring flight, a lady had a long layover at London's Heathrow Airport before the next portion of her journey. Buying a cup of coffee, a package of cookies, and the morning newspaper, she sat down at a table to enjoy all three. Soon she heard a rustling noise. Looking over her newspaper, she saw a young man helping himself to her cookies. She didn't want to make a scene, but neither did she want to lose all her cookies.

She leaned over and took a cookie. More rustling from the other side of the paper indicated that he had taken another too. Before long, just one cookie was left. He calmly broke it in two, pushed half toward her, ate his, and walked away.

She was still quietly fuming when her flight was called. She gathered up her stuff and found her bag of cookies. She had been eating his.

Of the two, which acted in gentleness and humility? Each of us needs to go and do the same. Working through the following questions will help you incorporate gentleness into your character.

BECOMING MORE MANLY

1. Have you had a recent experience like the author's at the football game, in which your gentleness was challenged? Describe it.

2. Of the four areas we most struggle to be gentle in (conflict, control, fear, self), which is most difficult for you? Explain.

3. What is your working definition of gentleness? Is it closer to the Bible's definition or to the world's?

4. On a scale of 1 to 5, with 1 representing "I have no gentleness" and 5 representing "I most often respond with gentleness," what would be your score? What would you like it to be?

5. Do you value gentleness as God does? How could you value it more?

6. In looking at how Moses and Jesus demonstrated gentleness, what most impresses you? Why?

7. Discuss the role our restraint plays in gentleness.

8. How can allowing God to guide your life build gentleness?

9. Discuss how courage and meekness relate to one another.

10. How is gentleness the opposite of selfishness?

11. What weeds most threaten to choke out gentleness in your life? What can you do to pull these weeds?

12. With your spouse or a close friend, talk over one decision you have made to allow gentleness to grow in your life. How can they help you in this? Be specific.

9
DOING WHAT WE MOST DESIRE
THE MANLY TRAIT OF SELF-CONTROL

The fruit of the Spirit is . . . self control.
Galatians 5:22-23

HER FACE AND NAME FADED LONG AGO. Where we met is equally unknown. Just a one-time date many years ago when I was single, but one memory remains fresh. I had mentioned to her something I wanted to do but wasn't able to.

She replied, "My big brother [her world revolved around her big brother and his marvelous wisdom] says we all do what we want."

I disagreed, somewhat strongly, as I recall. Perhaps I possessed some jealousy toward this unknown wise man; maybe it was just from my own tendency to take the opposite side just for discussion. (Friends tell me that trait is quite prominent!)

But after our discussion, I recognized the truth of what she said. We look at our options, weigh the benefits against the price we pay, and then do what we most want. If you tend to disagree with this concept, as I originally did, I merely ask you to think along with me for a short time.

A dental hygienist had a hard time removing the nicotine stains from a patient's teeth. The patient explained that she was trying to quit cigarettes but was having a difficult time. The hygienist revealed that she and her husband were trying to quit also and allowed themselves to smoke only outside the house. The patient thought it was a great idea and asked if it helped.

"Yes, but we're getting tired of watching TV through the patio doors."

That lady and her husband had figured out a way to do what they wanted, regardless of the consequences.

Do you do that? For several years I tried to get to the gym each morning by 7:00. I've learned that my aging body needs it. But I struggled, and I confess that it's been a long time since I made that trip. My bed hasn't abused me so badly that I want to leave it, especially to bring bodily pain and discomfort.

But I'll eagerly get up at 3:00 A.M. for a fishing trip. Why? Fishing is fun. I like fishing's relaxation much more than the pain of working out. Fishing is worth getting up for. I'm not so sure that working out is.

We do what we want.

One of the greatest dangers to our society, and particularly to the Church, is a lack of self-control—that is, self-control applied to what's good. We all seem to do fine with self-control on the "fun" things, like fishing. But self-control is a struggle for us all on the "good" things.

The growing debt spiral demonstrates that we want what we want when we want it. We find it difficult to say no to ourselves. We struggle even to say, "Later." A recent commercial for an agency that clears one's credit record proclaimed, "You deserve the American good life." What is that elusive "American good life"? The freedom never to have to say no to yourself. We guys fall prey to this. Have you heard the slogan that says, "The difference between men and boys is the price of their toys"?

Sexually, few people control their desires until marriage, including far too many Christians. Even in marriage, some don't always say no to their desires. One study revealed that 31 percent of married people commit adultery. Many don't control their anger. Violence increases at an alarming rate, especially in marriage.

God offers an alternative to Christian men, to implant His own character trait of self-control into our character. From the Holy Spirit living within, we can imbed self-control deep down inside. But self-control goes against our grain.

OUR NATURAL TENDENCY

We often tend to go with whatever is easiest. While in the Sierra Nevada Mountains, my dad and I fished the Owens River, a slow stream meandering through cow pastures and sage brush. During our drive there, a local radio station broadcast this quote: "Following the path of least resistance tends to make men, women, and rivers crooked."

The crookedness of the Owens River demonstrated the last part of that truth. A lack of self-control shows the first part is true also. The need for self-control impacts two main areas: (1) doing harmful things and (2) doing good things improperly.

DOING HARMFUL THINGS

All temptations promise fun, pleasure, and some benefit to us. Without that promise, we wouldn't do them so often. But if we don't control ourselves, the long-term price exceeds the benefits. The Bible calls these sin, because any use of them, even in the slightest amount, violates God's moral law.

Even more significant than violating morality, each sin has buried within itself the seed of destruction. That's why God prohibits these—not to arbitrarily see if we'll obey on unimportant matters, but to protect us.

Sex outside of marriage leads to the breakdown of the family as the key building block for society. Adultery destroys the trust necessary for true intimacy. Lying eliminates the honesty necessary for people to work together. We men face a particular vulnerability here, don't we?

With these acts, we need to use self-control at all times, because their wrongness is clear. Unfortunately, the frequency with which we do them is equally clear. It seems that today, acts considered sinful 25 years ago are now held up as praiseworthy, or merely as an alternative lifestyle. We see so many examples of people not exerting self-control here.

But the other area can be even more difficult to exert self-control in.

DOING GOOD THINGS EXCESSIVELY

When properly used, many things are necessary for life, bring godly pleasure, and are good. But if we don't practice self-control with them, they can become deadly issues of sin. When out of balance, they can control our lives and become our gods. That's the message Paul gave in Phil. 3:18-19, when writing to believers:

As I have often told you before and now say again with tears, many live as enemies of the cross of Christ. Their destiny is destruction, *their god is their stomach*, and their glory is in their shame. Their mind is on earthly things (emphasis added).

Notice the semi-hidden warning in the middle. When we allow ourselves to use good things excessively, like our appetite for food, these "good things" can become our gods. They become the main desire of our lives and can possess us. Our stomach, our sexual organs, or our beds can become our gods.

We need food, but when done to excess, it's gluttony. The proper use of sex is a tremendous joy and blessing, but outside marriage it's immorality. We need rest and leisure, but too much is laziness. We need to earn money to live, but we can slip over the line into greed.

Almost any good thing can be abused if we don't exert self-control. The core of the problem is that these aren't morally wrong. The problem comes when we don't employ self-control. So since the problem arises from within, the solution also arises from within.

The lack of self-control is a spiritual issue, solved only when we value and practice it until it becomes imbedded in our character. We can never be the person God designed us to be until we have godly self-control.

THE MANLY TRAIT OF SELF-CONTROL

Paul uses athletic imagery in 1 Cor. 9:24-27 to describe the need for self-control in the Christian life. Paul loved sports and frequently used sports examples. Perhaps he competed earlier in his life; he certainly knew the language and training techniques of the day. He probably attended athletic events when possible.

Although the term "self-control" isn't found in these verses, the concept certainly is. Here we find the two primary components of godly self-control. After we examine these two, we'll distill a definition.

Do you not know that in a race all the runners run, but only one gets the prize? Run in such a way as to get the prize. Everyone who competes in the games goes into strict training [self-control]. They do it to get a crown that will not last; but we do it [self-control] to get a crown that will last forever. Therefore I do not run like a man running aimlessly; I do not fight like a man beating the air. No, I beat my body and make it my slave [self-control] so that after I have preached to others, I myself will not be disqualified for the prize (*1 Cor. 9:24-27*, emphasis added).

This passage gives the first component of self-control, our desire for God's best in our lives.

A COMPELLING GOAL

All run in the race of life, but only a few run with passion. We begin to cultivate the character trait of self-control when we have a goal important enough that we must use self-control to arrange our lives to reach that goal. That's what Paul meant in verse 24: run to get the prize. Pay the price. The goal is worth it.

The Olympics demonstrates that vividly. Young athletes give up their normal social lives to practice hours a day, on top of their schooling. Some even leave their families to live and train with the best coaches in hopes they'll be the one person out of hundreds to win the gold.

We develop the character of God when we embrace a goal that will capture our lives, like having a passion to know God. All that we do should flow from that ambition. Remember—we do what we want.

We need to want righteousness enough to resist sexual temptation, a healthy body enough to resist overeating and insufficient exercise, Bible knowledge enough to commit time to study, our friends to come to Christ enough to risk their disapproval. That principle applies to each aspect of the Christian life.

If we don't fight temptation, or eat right, or study, or share Christ, what conclusion can be drawn except that those things really aren't that important to us? What power can keep us from doing them? Remember Phil. 4:13—"I can do everything through him who gives me strength."

Paul exhorts us not to just jog in the race of life, not to amble along. Grab life by the throat, seize the day, grab all the gusto you can, go for the gold. Choose a goal for life so great that you need to control your life to get it.

Athletes do that for a temporary prize, according to verse 25. Today's Olympic gold medal winners have a moment of glory. But can you name three gold medal winners from the last Games?

If we're willing to go for godly gold, the prize available to us is eternal life with God. We have the victorious life now and heaven later. That's the first part of self-control; the second part is to act on that desire.

CONSISTENT EFFORTS

Clearly, half-hearted efforts to reach all that God has intended for us won't achieve our goal. Just as receiving an Olympic gold medal requires great effort, so does receiving God's awesome prize—not working to earn the prize, but working in co-operation with Him.

Isn't that what Paul said in 1 Cor. 9:27 about conquering his body through self-control so he wouldn't be disqualified for the prize? Spiritual diligence, struggle, and self-control are vital.

Again, athletes do that. They go into strict training, diet, exercise, and practice. They build their lives to reach their goals. They eliminate anything that might deter them. And their goals don't begin to match ours.

Each time the Olympics begins, I dream of being one of the athletes. OK, I'm a little over the age range, but allow me to dream! But even apart from the age factor, I realize that the dream is just not worth the price. I have better things to give my life to. Achieving God's best for my life requires the same difficult and consistent efforts that athletes give. Being lackadaisical won't make it, according to Heb. 11:6—"Without faith it is impossible to please God, because anyone who comes to him must believe that he exists and that he rewards those who earnestly seek him."

How do we find God's best for us? By seeking God with earnestness, by shaping our lives to best reach our goals, to do what we most want to do. Back in the 1 Corinthians passage, Paul didn't aimlessly run in place—he ran for the finish line. He didn't shadow box—he went for the knockout. He wanted to use all his energy to accomplish something: the prize of knowing God.

To do that, he "beat" his body and made it his slave. That doesn't mean he physically abused his body but that he said no to its desires. He didn't let his physical desires drive his life. Through discipline and self-control, he took charge of his body to accomplish what he most wanted.

I'm sure part of him wanted to sleep in. As an apparently single man, part of him probably wanted to take advantage of the free sex that Corinth was famous for. Part of him assuredly said, "Paul, use your learning and intellect to build a secure retirement."

But Paul consistently made the efforts needed to train himself in self-control and godliness—not merely as a wish but as something he acted on. Wishes alone get us nowhere. Remember the old line "If wishes were horses, then beggars would ride"? If we want to ride, we need to add will to our wish.

If we desire self-control, we need a compelling goal to build our lives around. And we need consistent efforts to reach that goal. Now let me synthesize all we've said, to give a simple definition of self-control.

SELF-CONTROL DEFINED

Self-control is choosing a godly goal for our lives and doing whatever it takes to reach it. I don't know who he is, but an author named "Anonymous" has written a lot of good stuff. Here's one of his or her better works.

> Self-control is what transforms a promise into reality. It is the words that speak boldly of your intentions and the actions that speak louder than words. It is making the time when there is none, coming through time after time, year after year. Self-control is the stuff character is made of; the power to change the face of things. It is the daily triumph of integrity over skepticism.

Godly self-control wants God above all, coupled with a willingness to do what He requires to gain His best. This isn't based on our own willpower and determination. Rather, the character trait of self-control comes from our decision to value God and to use His power to make our changes.

God won't do it for us until we make the first step. Self-control means stepping off wherever God says step, even when we can't see what's next. Self-control chooses to do whatever God tells us, even when it seems impossible and doesn't make sense to us—especially when it's the opposite of what we would prefer to do.

Self-control desires the best, even when it's difficult and we would rather take it easy. Self-control requires continuing, when we would rather quit. Self-control puts God first when we would rather reign on the throne.

Self-control doesn't come easy for most of us. That's why God provides it as a trait of His that He wants to help us develop in our character.

CULTIVATING THE MANLY TRAIT OF SELF-CONTROL

Remember the people described in Phil. 3:18, who served themselves and their natural appetites? Without self-control, they couldn't seek God or experience His abundance. In verses 12-14 we find a contrasting life, *with* self-control:

Not that I have already obtained all this, or have already been made perfect, but *I press on* to take hold of that for which Christ Jesus took hold of me. Brothers, I do not consider myself yet to have taken hold of it. *But one thing I do:* Forgetting what is behind and *straining toward* what is ahead, *I press on* toward the goal *to win the prize* for which God has called me heavenward in Christ Jesus" (emphasis added).

Notice the order Paul gave. First, he recognized that he wasn't there yet. He wanted to be, but he wasn't quite there yet. To get there, he first had to give up some things. That meant that he intentionally forgot anything in the past that would be an obstacle. Second, he pressed on toward the goal. He worked hard at what was most important. He had a consuming passion to reach the prize.

In other words, Paul cultivated self-control. He put all his energy into his efforts. He carefully crafted his life to be most effective. If we desire to develop self-control in our lives, we must do the same. ·

NURTURE THE FRUIT OF SELF-CONTROL

Paul did a masterful job at "forgetting what is past" in order to "press on toward the goal to win the prize." But he didn't just eliminate weeds—he added a goal. To nurture self-control, we also need to establish a purpose in life, a purpose with enough passion to guide all we do.

Choose Your Goal

Many life goals alluringly beckon us: taking it easy, being comfortable, being financially secure, making it to the top of our profession, meeting our physical desires, being respected and admired by others.

But for Christians, our life goal comes with the name of our Savior: Jesus Christ. In Phil. 3 Paul revealed that his life goal was to be in heaven with Jesus. He ruthlessly eliminated anything that would work against that, courageously added anything that would help it, and sacrificially controlled his body and desires.

Valuing God so highly gave Paul the motivation for self-control. Wanting God more than all else gives us the power to do the same. Jesus was asked in Matt. 22:37-38 about what's most important in the godly life. He responded by describing the normal Christian life.

Love the Lord your God with all your heart and with all your soul and with all your mind. This is the first and greatest commandment.

We call that passion—a passion that drives all we do. We don't have to be intelligent, talented, or gifted. In the kingdom of God, the best ability is availability—availability to God with a passion to be used however He desires, willing to do whatever it takes, whatever the difficulty, whatever the sacrifice.

We face character decisions every day. Which act is most moral? Which best expresses godly self-control? Those decisions must be evaluated by the questions "Which of these will bring me closer to my life goal? Which will pull me away from it?" Then we make our decision and choose our action on that basis. Once we've decided to say no to self, once we've established a life goal, then we need to say yes to whatever helps us achieve that.

Just Say Yes

Self-control involves acting on whatever moves us closer to our godly goal. Remember the athletes of Paul's day in 1 Corinthians? They paid the price of training, proper diet, exercise, and practice. Their goal was temporary: a wreath of laurel that soon perished. But they had a goal and did all they could to reach it.

We also need to say yes to things that may decrease our leisure time, our financial security, our comfort. For each of us, the mix will be different. We begin as different individuals—we have different functions and ministries, different talents and energy levels.

As a result, exactly how we say yes will vary. But the process is the same. We build self-control deep down into our character as we decide that knowing and growing in God is more important to us than anything else in life. Then we continue to craft our lives to express that.

We say no to anything that hinders our goal. We say yes to anything that advances it. And we continue to do that until the tendency becomes a trait, until we have self-control imbedded in our character.

Working through the following questions should help you to choose self-control and begin developing it in your life.

BECOMING MORE MANLY

1. In the physical arena, what area do you struggle in to exert self-control?

2. If it's true that we do what we most desire, what would others say is most important to you? Are you happy with that answer?

3. Of the two areas requiring self-control (doing wrong things, doing good things excessively), which is most difficult for you?

4. What is your working definition of self-control? Is it closer to the Bible's definition or to the world's?

5. On a scale of 1 to 5, with 1 representing "I have no self-control" and 5 representing "I most often respond with self-control," what would be your score? What would you like it to be?

6. What weeds most threaten to choke out self-control in your life? What can you do to pull these weeds?

7. What good thing could you accomplish in the next month if you said no to some harmful or excessive things in your life?

8. What is the driving passion of your life? Do you have one? If not, develop a one-sentence passion statement that will give direction to your life.

9. What action steps can you take this week to carry out your passion statement?

10. What would God most want you to say yes to in the next month?

11. With your small group, spouse, or a close friend, talk over one decision you have made to allow self-control to grow in your life. How can they help you in this? Be specific.

10
GRABBING GOD'S GUSTO
BEING FILLED WITH THE SPIRIT

Live by the Spirit.
Galatians 5:16

MY FINGERS FORMED AN IMAGINARY GUN and pointed it at my four-year-old grandson.

"Stick 'em up!" I said.

An eager smile spread across Joshua's face as his hands shot into the sky. He waited.

"Jump up two times," was the next command, and his one-year-old sister, Hannah, giggled as her brother jumped to the sky.

"Now, hug your Grandma and give her a kiss." Both grandmother and grandson enjoyed that one.

"Next, make a funny face at Hannah." The contortions of his face matched her grin of glee at seeing her older brother act so silly.

The game continued until all of us ran out of ideas, and we moved on to another activity, but I discovered something about Joshua that day. He had quickly learned that "Stick 'em up" meant surrender, that you obey the person you raise your hands to.

That wasn't natural for Josh. The week before was the first time he told me to "Stick 'em up." I did, and he shot me! I explained how it worked, that raising your hands meant you give up—in exchange for not being shot. You obey as a substitute for death.

With our games that day, my grandson demonstrated to me a secret about deep-down character change. Many of us raise our hands in worship. Whether we do it physically or symbolically, it serves as a sign of surrender to God. We surrender in exchange for eternal life. But do we *truly* give up our lives to God? Only as we fully surrender can we receive the deep-down character change we've been talking about.

We've spent much time looking at the need for us to work with God in changing who we are. We've examined in depth the process of how to incorporate the nine character traits of God. One thing yet remains: to do what we've spent so much time talking about!—or to surrender fully to being the person God created us to be.

Have you ever wondered why some Christians are on fire for God and why others just smolder? They attend, they serve, they give, but they never seem to get it. They don't dig deep into God but merely dabble at the surface of faith. Their faith is genuine, they love God, but clearly something's missing.

Other Christians are different. They're not more talented or intelligent, but their lives have a zest for God. Passion motivates their actions. In the midst of real difficulties, their smiles reflect inner joy. Real changes are going on in them; deep-down character change is taking place.

What's the difference? Why do some Christians have gusto in their faith, and others don't? Why do some make the character changes we've talked about, while others just stay the same? That's the problem we'll address in this final chapter. I think that at least in part, this is a gender issue. Most churches have more women attenders than men. They have more women workers than men. They have more women who pray vigorously than men.

To paraphrase Thoreau, any semi-astute observer would see that many Christian men "lead lives of quiet mediocrity."

OUR NATURAL TENDENCY: BORING CHRISTIANITY

For many men, Christianity is a duty—a good and necessary duty but not something to get excited about. According to 1 Cor. 3:1-3, many allow themselves to be pulled in two directions:

> Brothers, I could not address you as spiritual but as worldly—mere infants in Christ. I gave you milk, not solid

food, for you were not yet ready for it. Indeed, you are still not ready. You are still worldly. For since there is jealousy and quarreling among you, are you not worldly?"

Remember that Paul is addressing Christians—the word "brothers" makes that obvious. Yet they were in two groups, spiritual Christians and worldly Christians. The worldly ones grabbed onto God with one hand and to the world with the other. They hadn't fully surrendered to God.

As a result of their indecision, they missed out on the best Paul had to offer: solid food rather than the bland milk for spiritual babies. Because they weren't willing to let go of the world, they could make little progress toward closeness with God.

Bart was an intelligent and cautious fourth-grader from the city who spent one summer visiting his country cousins. When they asked if he wanted to ride their horse Champ, Bart jumped at the chance.

Up close, the horse was much larger than horses Bart had seen in cowboy movies. Deciding to get on the horse one small step at a time, he climbed onto a rail fence next to the horse in order to mount him. With one foot firmly planted on the fence, Bart threw his other foot over the saddle.

For Champ, this was a new way to be mounted, and he didn't quite know what to make of this strange event. He slowly moved away from the fence, pulling part of Bart with him. Bart's caution kept him on the fence; his desire for adventure kept him on the horse—for a short time only, though.

His eight-year-old legs couldn't stretch forever, and he was soon deposited on the pasture ground, which was filled with what pastures are usually filled with. Why did he fall? He wasn't willing to fully surrender to the process of getting on the horse.

The Christian is the same. If we try to hold on to both the world and God, we fall into bad stuff. These Corinthian Christians were quite a bit like many of the people we see in church each week.

Jesus described such persons in an even more vivid manner in Rev. 3:15-16. They're halfhearted, and just half a heart won't pump the spiritual blood of Christ.

I know your deeds, that you are neither cold nor hot. I wish you were either one or the other! So, because you are lukewarm—neither hot nor cold—I am about to spit you out of my mouth.

If you asked these church members in Laodicea, I'm sure they would have proclaimed both allegiance to and love of Christ. But to Christ that wasn't enough. He wants fire in our souls that shows on the outside. He wants us to have passion for being transformed into His character.

He requires holiness and passion. He requires transformation, and transformation requires surrender. Surrendering to God gives us the motivation and power for deep-down character change.

MANLY CHARACTER CHANGE: POWERED BY GUSTO

Remember—our goal is deep-down character change. Let's work backward to see how we arrive there. Achieving such a dramatic transformation of our character requires a strong motivation. Only an intense passion for God can provide that desire to change. How do we build that gusto for God?

Spiritual gusto comes when we surrender fully to God, when we accept both God's goals and methods for our lives, when we get off the fence that Bart wanted to stay anchored to and jump onto the horse.

We can quickly summarize the process. Surrender to God produces passion, passion then produces the motivation for deep-down character change. Surrender, then passion, then change. Passion, or gusto, is the balancing point between surrender and change.

Spiritual gusto comes after we choose to be single-minded in our pursuit of God—when we want God above all else, when we don't want to hold on to the world and God at the same time, when we're willing to go anywhere and be anything God desires, when we want to incorporate God's character into ours.

The Bible calls that being led by or filled with the Holy Spirit. Only when the Spirit fills us can His fruit flourish in us. In our main text on the fruit of the Spirit, Paul the Apostle gives a powerful description of the distinction between the Spirit-led life and the self-led life. Let's go back to a portion of that text:

> Those who belong to Christ Jesus have crucified the sinful nature with *its passions and desires*. Since we live by the Spirit, let us keep in step with the Spirit. . . . *Live by the Spirit*, and you will not gratify the desires of the sinful nature. For the sinful nature desires what is contrary to the Spirit, and the Spirit what is contrary to the sinful nature. *They are in conflict with one another*, so that you do not do what you want (*Gal. 5:24-25; 16-17,* emphasis added).

According to Paul, what is the solution to being torn in two directions? To surrender to God, or to allow God's Spirit to lead you in one direction, one step at a time. Notice also the warning: either we gratify our sinful nature, or we gratify God's Holy Spirit. We can't do both, and our degree of passion for God comes from that choice.

The true Christian wants God and His righteousness more than anything. The true Christian wants to nurture the character of God within.

When we have this single-minded dedication to God, we build passion and gusto. That will then give us the motivation to cooperate with God in finishing the character changes He began in us.

When we allow the Holy Spirit to guide each step of our lives, we then have that single-minded devotion, which I call gusto and passion. Only when we allow the Holy Spirit to fill us can He transform our character deep down. For the fruit of the Spirit to flourish in us, we must allow that same Spirit to fill every nook and cranny of our lives.

BEING FILLED WITH THE SPIRIT

I'm intrigued by the way God puts things together. On the day of Pentecost, described in Acts 2:1-4, the sound of a violent wind was heard, tongues of fire touched the heads of the disciples, they were filled with the Holy Spirit. This created such a stir that a crowd of thousands rushed to check out the situation.

When they saw these marvelous things, how did they respond? Look at verse 13: "Some, however, made fun of them and said, 'They have had too much wine.'"

I once heard a sermon entitled "Are You Drunk Enough?" The title alone caught my attention, and the content intrigued me. The sermon, of course, was about giving control to the Holy Spirit.

LOSS OF CONTROL

Losing control to the Spirit means allowing the Holy Spirit to choose our steps rather than choosing all of them ourselves. When we walk with the Spirit, we experience a yielding of control.

EXUBERANCE

Second, we experience exuberance when we give the Holy Spirit control. Being filled with the Holy Spirit gives us an unexplainable joy that enables us to smile, even in the worst of times. We don't worry about pleasing people, just pleasing God, and that is very freeing. Non-Christians just can't understand our joy, which comes from the Spirit.

ADDICTIVE

Being filled with the Spirit also hooks us. Once we've had a taste of the love, joy, and power the Holy Spirit brings to our lives, we want more! Why would anyone want to go back to a lukewarm walk with God once he or she has experienced spiritual ecstasy?

As we allow ourselves to be filled with the Spirit, as we allow Him to guide each step, we move away from being pulled in two directions. We move away from being lukewarm. We cooperate with God to make the changes needed to be who He designed us to be.

When we're filled with the Spirit, we want more of God. We realize that to get more of God, He needs to get more of us. This is how we grab God's gusto, how we build a passion to get deeper into changing our character.

BEING FILLED

Being filled with the Spirit means we yield our lives to God. That's the surrender we talked of with my grandson Joshua, to put God in first place in our lives.

Being filled allows the Holy Spirit access to all our hidden rooms. Some time ago, we had some close friends over for a Christmas dinner. However, we had half a dozen different projects going on simultaneously and couldn't finish them all beforehand, so we thoroughly cleaned the house only after putting all the loose ends of our projects in the study.

The house was neat, clean, dusted, freshly vacuumed—and the study doors were firmly shut! No one would guess that to walk into the study meant to take your life in your own hands. Sometimes our spiritual lives are like that, aren't they? Inviting Jesus into our lives is somewhat like inviting Him into our house. We've cleaned up all the main rooms. At first glance, everything looks pretty good.

But we have a secret junk room where we hide thoughts and acts we want no one to see. We may even try to deny their existence to ourselves. Usually those doors have a master lock that would withstand a .357 magnum bullet, like the one in the commercial.

Being filled with the Holy Spirit means we unlock those locks and allow God to open the doors. I encourage you to think carefully now about your closets, what you're trying to hide from the God who loves you as you are, who wants to transform your character.

Being filled with the Spirit means letting God's presence and character fill us. More than anything, we want what He wants.

We've seen that being filled with the Holy Spirit is essential to character change, and we've seen what it means. Now, how do we do it? How do we open up all those rooms we've locked?

If we desire the Holy Spirit to fill us, we must remember He's called the *Holy* Spirit for a reason. We can't be filled with the Holy Spirit without a deep-seated desire to be holy. Holiness means pursuing righteousness with passion and allowing God to move us away from sin in thought and deed.

A missionary worked with a tribe in Africa, and some became Christians. The tribal chief didn't accept Christ, but he closely watched how some experienced a real transformation while others showed no change. He finally declared, "If being a

Christian makes you a better person, you may remain so. If not, I forbid you to be a Christian at all!"

That unbelieving chief had a clear idea of what Christianity is all about: an inner character change that expresses itself in our behavior. We move away from sin and embrace holiness. Without knowing the dynamics, that chief understood that character change accompanies genuine conversion.

Being filled with the Holy Spirit requires a heartfelt commitment to move away from sin and toward righteousness. According to John 16:8, one of the main roles of the Holy Spirit is to convict people of sin.

How can we be filled with this Holy Spirit if we want to maintain sin in our life at the same time? How can we be led by the Spirit, if we continually turn away from His holiness toward sin? Do you see the problem?

According to Acts 2:38, just to receive the Spirit, we need to repent, or to turn away from sin. How much more must we turn away from sin if we want the Spirit to fill us? So once we've asked to be filled with the Spirit, to receive that filling we must turn away from sin.

If we won't repent, we can't be filled with the Holy Spirit. We cultivate the gusto in our lives that will produce deep-down character change when we turn away from our old selves and cooperate with God to become new. That allows the Holy Spirit to fill us.

CUT LOOSE

Clearly, the Holy Spirit wants to spark a fire in us. Our job is to be sure we don't dampen that fire, that we burn with passion for God. What does all this mean?

It means that we don't fight against what the Holy Spirit wants to accomplish in our lives. Part of that certainly includes character transformation. This means that we don't look at the bottom line before we obey, that we don't search for reasons to say no. Rather, when God speaks to us, we look for reasons to say yes.

The pastor in me requires that I caution that we be sure it truly is God speaking to us! Too many excesses are attributed to God, which instead should be blamed on either immaturity or wanting to "hear" God say something that we already desire.

The Holy Spirit primarily leads from His book: the Bible. We need to study to ensure that where we believe the Spirit leads us squares with the Word.

Then, once we're sure it's the Holy Spirit speaking to us, we cut loose, or we relax our inhibitions regarding following God and do it. We keep in step with the Spirit, according to Gal. 5:25. We don't jump ahead; we don't fall behind.

That's what it means to be filled with the Spirit. That's the source of gusto in our faith. And that's the key to our deep-down character change. We'll only experience exuberance in our faith when we attempt something so great that if God isn't in it, we're sure to fail.

COMMIT TO BEING FILLED WITH THE SPIRIT

Attempting to change our character will fail, unless we open our lives fully to God. That was the lesson I learned more than 20 years ago when I tried to make those changes on my own and couldn't.

But when you yield yourself to God's Spirit, who lives within you, when you allow Him to develop His fruit in your character, then you'll become a different person. You'll experience spiritual ecstasy. You'll be the person God designed you to be. Henry Varley said, "The world has yet to see what God will do with a man who is fully and wholly consecrated to the Holy Spirit."

I challenge you—ask God to fill you with His Spirit, and commit your life to holiness. Commit yourself to deep-down character change. That change can come only from surrendering to whatever the Holy Spirit asks of you. Let Him both fill and lead you. As you do, your passion for God will grow.

God never asks of us what he doesn't enable us to do. You might want to memorize Phil. 4:13 as an encouragement for the times when the road gets difficult—"I can do everything through him who gives me strength." With the Holy Spirit living within, providing power, and filling you, you can accomplish all God has in store for you.

Right now, ask God to fill you with His Holy Spirit and begin this tremendous adventure.